BADMINTON

BROWN

PHYSICAL EDUCATION ACTIVITIES SERIES

Consulting Editor:

AILEENE LOCKHART
University of Southern California
Los Angeles, California

Evaluation Materials Editor:

JANE A. MOTT
Smith College
Northampton, Massachusetts

ARCHERY, Wayne C. McKinney
BADMINTON, Margaret Varner
BIOPHYSICAL VALUES OF MUSCULAR ACTIVITY, E. C. Davis, Gene A. Logan, and Wayne C. McKinney
BOWLING, Joan Martin
CIRCUIT TRAINING, Robert P. Sorani
CONDITIONING FOR WOMEN, Jane A. Mott
CONTEMPORARY SQUARE DANCE, Patricia A. Phillips
FENCING, Muriel Bower and Torao Mori
FIELD HOCKEY, Anne Delano
GOLF, Virginia L. Nance and E. C. Davis
HANDBALL, Michael Yessis
MEN'S BASKETBALL, Glenn Wilkes
MEN'S GYMNASTICS, A. Bruce Frederick
MODERN DANCE, Esther E. Pease
PHYSICAL AND PHYSIOLOGICAL CONDITIONING FOR MEN, Benjamin Ricci
SKIING, Clayne Jensen and Karl Tucker
SKIN AND SCUBA DIVING, Albert A. Tillman
SOCCER, Richard L. Nelson
SOCIAL DANCE, William F. Pillich
SOFTBALL, Marian E. Kneer and Charles L. McCord
SQUASH RACQUETS, Margaret Varner and Norman Bramall
SWIMMING, Betty J. Vickers and William J. Vincent
TABLE TENNIS, Margaret Varner and J. R. Harrison
TENNIS, Joan Johnson and Paul Xanthos
TRACK AND FIELD, Kenneth E. Foreman and Virginia L. Husted
TRAMPOLINING, Jeff T. Hennessy
VOLLEYBALL, Glen H. Egstrom and Frances Schaafsma
WEIGHT TRAINING, Philip J. Rasch
WOMEN'S BASKETBALL, Frances Schaafsma
WOMEN'S GYMNASTICS, A. Bruce Frederick
WRESTLING, Arnold Umbach and Warren R. Johnson

PHYSICAL EDUCATION

ACTIVITIES SERIES

BADMINTON

MARGARET VARNER

University of Delaware

WM. C. BROWN COMPANY PUBLISHERS

DUBUQUE, IOWA

Manufactured by WM. C. BROWN CO. INC., Dubuque, Iowa
Printed in U. S. A.

Foreword

I consider it both a privilege and a delight to contribute the Foreword to this excellent textbook entitled *Introduction to Badminton* by its distinguished author, Margaret Varner. She is admirably qualified through personal endowment, educational background, and illustrious experience to contribute to the relatively meager professional literature in the area of this very important and increasingly popular sport for both sexes and all ages.

We are all familiar with the specious, though sometimes true, cliché to the effect that "Those who *can*, do and those who *cannot*, teach." It is a statement all too generally accepted in its glorification of the performer and correlative scorn of the teacher. It is most gratifying, therefore, to have an opportunity to refute this arrogant and false idea with respect to the particular author of this particular textbook.

Margaret Varner's formidable list of national and international championships in badminton, tennis, and squash racquets is indisputable proof that she can *do*. This "doing," however, is coupled with her outstanding prestige as a master teacher. With both a Bachelor's and a Master of Arts degree with a major sequence in physical education, Miss Varner has had approximately fifteen years of highly successful teaching experience. Her respect for her subject matter area and her eagerness that others share the richness of her experiences are attested to by the admiration and respect of many hundreds of students who have had the benefit of her tutelage.

We in physical education are deeply concerned with inculcating in our students the true understanding of sportsmanship in its broad, cultural sense, embracing both manners and morals. The impeccable example set by Miss Varner in this kind of sportsmanship is of inestimable value through the continuing momentum of its influence in our field. That we teach by example as well as by precept is only another way of saying that an individual teaches what he or she is.

We in the College of Health, Physical Education and Recreation at the Texas Woman's University are proud to pay tribute to a beloved author, artist-teacher and sportswoman, par excellence.

Anne Schley Duggan, Dean
College of Health, Physical Education and Recreation
Texas Woman's University
Denton, Texas

Preface

The purpose of this book is to provide both the beginning and advanced badminton player with an organized description of how best to perform and enjoy the game. The real student of badminton must not only learn *how* to execute fundamental techniques but he should learn *when* and *why* they should be employed. These questions are discussed herein. Instructions and analyses are accompanied by sequence photographs and illustrative diagrams. Practice drills are outlined. A glossary of terms peculiar to badminton, a section on equipment, a description of badminton associations and tournaments, and a bibliography constitute a handy reference for the enthusiast.

Self-evaluation questions are distributed throughout the text. These afford the reader typical examples of the kinds of understanding and levels of skill that he should be acquiring as he progresses toward mastery of badminton. The player should not only answer the printed questions but should pose additional ones as a self-check on learning. Since the order in which the content of the text is read and the teaching progression of the instructor are matters of individual decision, the evaluative materials are not positioned according to the presentation of given topics. In some instances the student may find that he cannot respond fully and accurately to a question until he has read more extensively or has gained more playing experience. From time to time he should return to such troublesome questions until he is sure of the answers or has developed the skills called for, as the case may be.

Although this book is designed primarily for college physical education classes, the information is clearly suitable for and useful to the back yard, club, or tournament player.

Contents

What Badminton Is Like

Badminton is a game played with rackets and shuttlecocks on a court divided by a net. The game, which gets it name from an English estate, appears to have been played in India and England in the mid and late nineteenth century. Since that time, badminton has enjoyed considerable popularity in many countries.

Badminton can be played indoors or outdoors, with artificial or natural lighting. There may be two players on a side (the four-handed or doubles game) or one player on a side (the two-handed or singles game). The shuttlecock does not bounce; therefore it is played in the air, making for an exceptionally fast game requiring quick reflexes and superb conditioning. There is a wide variety of strokes in the game ranging from powerfully hit smashes to delicately played dropshots.

The measurements of the singles and doubles courts are shown in Figures 1 and 2. The court is bisected by a net 5′ from the ground at the center and 5′1″ at the posts, which are situated on the doubles sidelines. When played indoors, the badminton hall should be not less than 25 ft. in height above the middle of the net. The shuttlecock (or shuttle) has from 14 to 16 feathers and weighs from 73 to 85 grains. The racket is light in weight, only 5 oz., and is strung with gut or nylon. Figure 3 shows a fine quality racket and shuttle.

A badminton game consists of 15 points, except in ladies singles which is 11 points. The best of three games constitutes a match. Occasionally a handicap game of 21 points is played, in which case one game completes a match. The right to choose ends or to serve or receive first in the first game of a match is decided by tossing. If the side winning the toss chooses to serve first, the other side chooses ends, and vice versa. The

1

sides change ends at the beginning of the second game and at the beginning of the third if a third game is necessary. In a 15 point game, ends are changed in the third game when the leading side reaches eight; in an 11 point game when either side reaches 6, ends are changed. The side that wins a game serves first in the next game.

When the score is "13 all" in singles and doubles games which consist of 15 points, the side which reached 13 first has the option of "setting" the

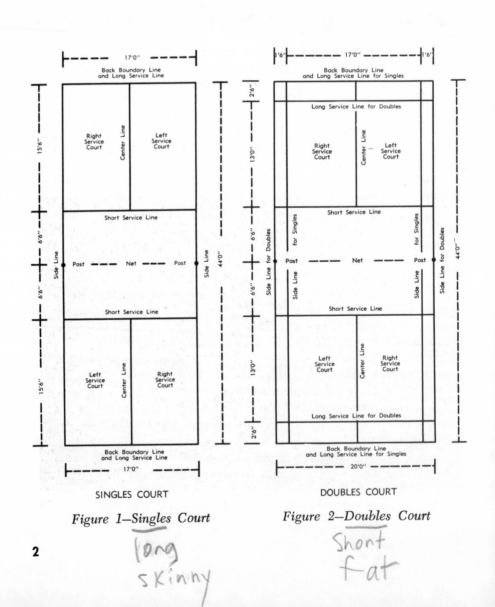

SINGLES COURT   DOUBLES COURT

Figure 1—Singles Court   *Figure 2—Doubles Court*

game to 5, and the side that scores 5 points first wins the game. The score may be set in the same manner at "14 all" for 3 points. In ladies' singles, the 11 point game may be set at "9 all" for 3 points or "10 all" for 2 points.

The game is started with an underhand stroke (serve) by a player in the right service court serving to a player in the right service court diagonally opposite. After the serve is completed the shuttle is "in play" back and forth across the net until it touches the ground, goes into the net, or until some other fault occurs. Points can be scored only by the serving side.

In singles, if the server fails to win the point, the score remains the same; it is then "service over," and the opposing side gains the serve and the opportunity to score. When a player has scored an even number of points, the serve must be to the right service court; when the server's score is an odd number of points, the serve is always sent to the left service court. The receiver adjusts accordingly.

In doubles, only one partner of the side that starts a game has a turn at serving in the first inning; in every subsequent inning each player on each side has a turn, the partners serving consecutively. When a point is scored, the server changes courts and serves to the other service

Figure 3—Racket and Shuttlecock

3

court. Only the serving side changes service courts when a point is scored. The receivers remain in their same courts to allow the server to serve to the other player.

In addition to the service regulations, there are other rules to follow in playing the game, and certain terms to understand. These specifics are discussed in the chapter on rules.

Badminton has developed in popularity since its early beginnings. It has always been very well liked in the British Isles. Denmark, Sweden, and West Germany lead the European countries in their interest, whereas Malaysia, Indonesia, Thailand, and India practically consider badminton the national sport of their countries. The game spread to Canada and the United States where national organizations similar to those of other countries were formed. The number of clubs in the U.S. is, however, nowhere near the number found in the aforementioned countries. With increased leisure time, badminton will no doubt play an important role in the fitness and recreational programs so vital to the American citizen. It can be played by men, women, and children of all ages, indoors and outdoors, with a minimum of expense and effort. The game itself is stimulating mentally and physically, and it combines the values of individual and team sports. The fact that it can be learned easily makes it enjoyable from the outset. A "rally" is developed by most players on their first attempt at the game. Although basic techniques are easy to learn, much practice and concentration are needed to perfect the skills necessary to become a good player.

Skills
Essential for Everyone

Before attempting stroking technique, a player must learn how to grip his racket, where to position himself on the court, how to stand when awaiting returns, and how to move about the playing surface.

THE GRIPS (Figures 4 and 5)

Most badminton strokes are executed with either a forehand or backhand grip. Strokes made overhead or on the right side of the body require a forehand grip; strokes made on the left side of the body require a backhand grip. (All comments in this book refer to right-handed players; left-handed players should reverse the instructions.)

The forehand grip in badminton resembles the Eastern forehand grip in tennis in that the point of the "V" formed by the thumb and forefinger is on the top bevel of the eight-sided handle. In order to allow for wrist movement, hold the racket in the fingers rather than palm it. The handle lies diagonally across the fingers and palm allowing the little finger to maintain a firm hold. More wrist action is achieved if the racket is held as near the end as possible. The fingers, particularly the forefinger and third finger, are comfortably spread. Hold the racket firmly at impact when executing power shots and more loosely on "touch" shots.

To get a comfortable feeling it may be necessary to adjust this basic grip by spreading or closing the fingers, by moving the hand closer to the end, or by resting the end of the handle at a comfortable place on the heel of the hand. The position of the "V" should not change.

To take a backhand grip for shots played on the left side of the body, turn your hand counterclockwise until the point of the "V" is on

Under what circumstances and for whom do A,B,C,D,E represent the basic position?

Why is it desirable to return to the basic position after each stroke?

Evaluation Questions
BASIC POSITION

the top left bevel. Most important, place the ball of the thumb flat against the back bevel of the handle. This thumb position gives the support needed to gain speed on drives and depth on clears. Since dropshots and net shots demand control rather than power, it is not necessary to

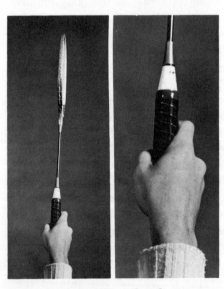 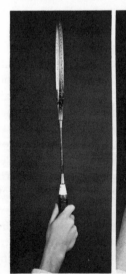

Figure 4—Forehand Grip   *Figure 5—Backhand Grip*

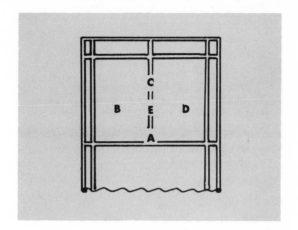

Diagram A:

BASIC POSITION

have the thumb flat; in fact, the side of the thumb may rest along the back bevel as it does on the forehand.

CENTER POSITION

The center or basic position is that location on the court from which you are able to reach most shots easily. It is equidistant from the net and back boundary line and equidistant from the sidelines. If you establish yourself in this position, you command the best area for any maneuver. Your opponent will try to draw you from this basic center position by directing the shuttle to a corner, thereby compelling you to move from the center of the court. Then, if he takes advantage of his corner placement, he will quickly exploit the open space. You must therefore retrieve the corner shots but recover quickly in order to return to the center position and close the space that was momentarily open. The basic position may be altered to some degree, depending upon your abilities and depending upon the position on the court from which your opponent is returning the shuttle (angle of return—See Chapter 5.) The more experience you gain playing badminton, the easier it will be for you to anticipate the returns. You will soon learn your opponent's strengths and weaknesses as well as your own, and your center location will adjust accordingly.

READY POSITION (Figure 6)

To ready yourself for each of your opponent's strokes, take a position in the center of the court and stand alertly with your weight evenly

7

Can you take a forehand grip and bounce the shuttle on the racket face without missing for 10, 15, and then 20 times?

With the same grip, can you alternate sides of the racket for each bounce?

Evaluation Questions

distributed on the balls of your feet. Your feet should be apart just enough to give good balance, and yet not so far apart that movement is restricted. Knees should be slightly flexed and easy, ready for instantaneous action. Your body is relaxed rather than stiff and upright. Both arms are carried in front of the body with the racket acting almost as a shield to keep the shuttle from getting past. The racket head is held up about shoulder height in front and away from the body to allow a swift strike. Experiment to determine the best position for you. Your eyes concentrate on the shuttle as it is leaving your opponent's racket, endeavoring to ascertain the direction of the attack or defense. As soon as the direction is determined, your feet move, and your body is pivoting by the time the shuttle crosses the net.

All players vary the ready position somewhat to suit their

Figure 6—Ready Position

own style and comfort; champions adjust it to give them the greatest mobility and quickness. Quickness refers not only to feet and hands but to eyes and brain as well. The shuttle has such a short distance to travel that it will come swiftly and give little time for you to execute the fundamentals. In fact, in badminton there is absolutely no time to pause and "survey" the situation. Even in doubles, where your partner covers half of the court, you have to be ready for every shot. Points are made because opponents have neither the time nor the reflexes to get their rackets in position to return the shuttle.

FOOTWORK

In order to get within reach of the shuttlecock, good footwork is essential. Powerful and deceptive strokes are of little use if a player is not in the correct place soon enough to stroke the shuttle effectively.

The beginning of good footwork is an alert starting position. Keep the body ready to move by flexing the knees slightly with the weight on the forward part of the feet and think "ready." A stiff upright stance does not indicate or permit speed. "Bouncing" best describes badminton footwork.

To move to the baseline, take a sideways skipping action with the feet kept close to the floor. To hit a forehand or overhead stroke in the deep right court, skip diagonally back to your right, with the right foot leading, and finish with the left side partially turned toward the net with the left foot forward. To play a backhand drive or clear from the deep left court, skip diagonally back, left foot leading, and with the right side to the net and the right foot diagonally forward.

Since it is a natural habit, the easiest part of badminton footwork is running forward. Because the basic waiting position is in the center of the court, however, backward and sideward steps are also required. The skill of moving backwards is called "back pedaling." It is a talent demanded in other sports, too. The "T" formation quarterback back pedals almost every time he takes the ball from center. His success as a quarterback is greatly dependent on his ability to move backwards without turning around; so it is with the badminton player. The head and eyes should be forward at all times. If a player has to turn and run with his back to the net, he will not have enough time to turn again to stroke the shuttle with ease. In fact, he will have to struggle to make the shot before it contacts the court.

The basic badminton strokes are the serve, the overhead clear, the dropshot, the overhead smash, and the drive. Note Figure 7. Except for the

Can you identify the foot position, A, B, or C that is correct for the forehand drive, the backhand drive, and the ready position?

Evaluation Questions
FOOTWORK

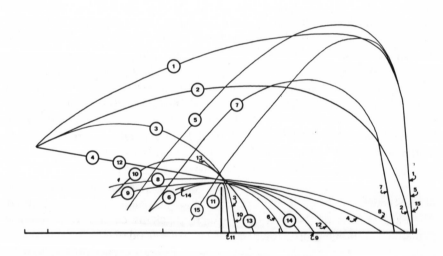

1. Defensive Clear
2. Attacking Clear
3. Overhead Dropshot
4. Smash
5. High Singles Serve
6. Low Doubles Serve
7. High Doubles Serve
8. Drive
9. Midcourt Drive
10. Underhand Dropshot
11. Hairpin Netshot
12. Half-Smash
13. Net Smash
14. Push Shot
15. Underhand Clear

Figure 7—Flight Patterns

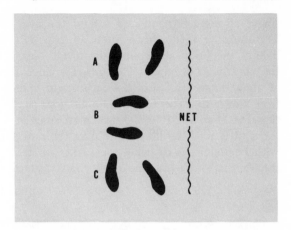

Diagram B:

FOOTWORK

serve, which is an underhand stroke, and the drive, which is a sidearm stroke, the overhead stroke preparations of the clear, drop, and smash should be as indistinguishable as possible. The fun of many games is to make use of the basic elements (strokes, in badminton) in such a way (strategy) that you outwit and deceive your opponent. Keep this in mind from the very beginning as you learn the strokes. Badminton is a game that epitomizes deception and your strokes should reflect this characteristic.

Your game will develop and grow, and your potential can be fulfilled sooner if thought and attention are given to the basic instructions in this chapter. Attention to detail describes the champion.

THE SERVE (Figure 8)

The serve is the underhand stroke that begins each play. Legally it can be played underhand forehand or underhand backhand, although underhand forehand is the usual method. The head of the racket must be below the server's hand at contact point, and the contact point must be below the waist.

To serve in singles, take a comfortable position in the court about three feet behind the short service line and to the right or left of the center line. Stand with your feet spread but not so far apart that you cannot move quickly. The left foot should be in advance of the right. A player's feet must remain in contact with the floor until the shuttle is contacted. Hold the shuttle at the base between the thumb and fore-

11

finger of the left hand and extend the arm out at about shoulder level. The racket is held with a forehand grip with the wrist cocked and taken behind the body at about waist level. This is the starting position; then the shuttle is dropped. The racket swings forward to the contact point at about knee level. Let the racket and shuttle meet ahead of and away from the body. The follow-through goes in the direction that you intend the shuttle to go. It will finish high since it is an underhand stroke and the shuttle must be hit up and over the net. A common mistake, especially with beginners, is to bring the racket up to the shuttle without dropping the shuttle. Such practice results in an outright miss or in a wood shot.

Figure 8—Serve

PLACEMENT AREAS (Figure 9)

As shown in Figure 7, the serve can be directed high or low, short or long. Figure 9 shows the specific areas within the service court to which

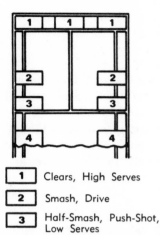

1	Clears, High Serves
2	Smash, Drive
3	Half-Smash, Push-Shot, Low Serves
4	Dropshots, Hairpin Net Shot

Figure 9—Placement Areas

the shuttle can be served most effectively. There should be no difference in the production of the low and high serves, as deception again is important in order to keep your opponent in doubt as to which it will be. Basically, the high serve is used more often in singles and the low serve more often in doubles. Occasionally mixing them keeps your opponent uncertain and unable to predict your pattern. It is imperative that you serve well, as serving gives you the opportunity to score.

Even though alike in production, the low and high serves are very different. They can be compared with the dropshot and clear with regard to wrist action and needed power. The low serve takes little power and is almost guided over the net whereas the high, deep serve will take all the strength and power available to get it high enough and deep enough to be considered successful. It has much the same flight as the clear because it is hit to a point high above the backcourt, and when it loses its speed, it turns and falls straight down. If it falls straight down on the back boundary line, the opponent must be that far back in the court to return it. If it is too flat and too low, the receiver will intercept it before it ever gets to the backcourt. On the other hand, the low serve has a flat arc as it just skims over the net and into the court near the short service line. A great deal less shoulder, arm, and wrist power will be needed to hit the short distance and low trajectory required for the low serve.

Because the serve is played underhand and therefore must be hit upward, it is considered a defensive stroke. Consequently, in order to score, the server must eventually turn his defense into an attack. Since the receiver cannot score a point, his objective is to stay on the attack and win the opportunity to serve, making it possible then for him to score. This peculiarity of badminton—having to score from a beginning defensive position—prolongs a game even though no points are recorded. Championship matches often illustrate this. In 1952, for example, two leading international players, Dave Freeman of the United States and Wong Peng Soon of Malaya played a Thomas Cup singles match. The final score was 15/4, 15/1 and the match took over an hour to complete. Both players must have been in superb physical condition and evenly matched, despite the fact that the final score gives no indication of such closeness.

THE OVERHEAD CLEAR (Figure 10)

The clear is a high shot to the back of the court; it may be offensive or defensive. Generally, offensive shots are hit down. The attacking clear is the exception to this rule.

To get a good clear, take the proper forehand grip, watch the approaching shuttle, use the prescribed footwork, and move yourself to a place where you are in the correct relationship to the shuttle. As you are moving to this position behind the shuttle, swing your racket and arm back behind the head and shoulders. This will require pivoting at the waist and turning the shoulders sideways to the net. The position is fundamentally the same as that used by a baseball fielder making an overarm throw to home plate. In badminton the racket, instead of the ball, is in the hand, but it is literally thrown at the shuttle in the identical fashion. As the racket moves from behind the head, the arm becomes fully extended at the contact point. Incorrectly allowing the arm to drop and bend when stroking results in loss of power. In addition, the extended arm gives great freedom of movement and the uninhibited and satisfying feeling of good clean stroking. The contact point is not directly above the head as overhead might imply; it is in front of you. Your ideal position is behind and in line with the shuttle. Overheads should be taken ahead at the soonest possible point of contact, and not be allowed to drop low and to the side. Consequently, always hit the shuttle as soon as possible so that your opponent will not have time to get to your shots. Meet the shuttle with a flat racket or surface without any cutting or slicing motion. Cutting gives control but takes away power.

In badminton, power is essential to send the clear high and deep. In addition, the shuttlecock is difficult to slice because of its feathers, and it does not react as a spinning ball does. Since you want the shuttle to go high and deep, the racket will swing forward and up, and the follow-through will simply follow the shuttle. In many strokes the purpose of the follow-through is to bring the shuttle down—but not in this instance. It could almost be said that there is no follow-through. The racket might finish pointing down because of the wrist snap, but the arm is not brought down purposely. The contact of the racket and shuttle must be quite explosive to get distance, since there is little weight in the racket. Note the flight of the clear in Figure 7. The shuttle is hit high enough so that at a certain point, almost above the back boundary line, it loses speed and turns and falls straight down. A shuttle falling per-

Evaluation Questions

Can you and your opponent rally the shuttle for 15, 20, and then 25 consecutive hits?

pendicular to the floor is most difficult to play. Very few people have power enough to smash a clear from the back boundary line. By the time the smash reaches the other side of the net, its speed is greatly diminished.

Figure 10—Overhead Clear

The high deep or defensive clear is used primarily to gain time to return to the center position in the court. One of the outstanding values of the high deep clear is in its use in combinations with the dropshot to run your opponent, making him defend all four corners of the court. As can be seen in Figure 7, depth and height of the shuttlecock on the defensive clear are extremely important in order to force your opponent as far to the backcourt as possible. Your next shot, a dropshot just over the net, would become very effective in this game of maneuvering for openings and spaces. It might also force your opponent to hit a short return which could be smashed. It takes a strong player to clear from one baseline to the other and an extraordinarily strong player to high clear to the diagonal corner. Unless a shuttle that flies very fast is used, it is unlikely that the average player would be able to accomplish this difficult feat. Consequently, in singles, the player who first hits a high deep defensive clear gains control of the rally and should eventually win that point. In analyzing a match played by contestants of equal skill, the player who consistently has good length always wins. When playing, if you find you do not have time to reach the shots and each point is a struggle, then check the length of your clears. Your opponent will seldom return a winning shot or putaway if your clear is deep enough. Clears that are too low and too short are cut off before they reach the backcourt.

After learning the basic high deep clear just described, a modification of this shot, the attacking clear, can be developed. Its use should not be confused with the uses of the defensive clear or disaster will result. The trajectory of the attacking clear is not as high but it is faster. There is a different arc to the flight pattern, as can be seen in Figure 7. Because it is low, the opponent must be drawn out of the center position before the attacking clear can be used successfully. Often it is best used following a good dropshot to the forehand corner. The clear can then be hit quickly to the backhand corner while the opponent is recovering from the net. Once the clear gets behind the opponent on the backhand, the return is almost sure to be in the forecourt. When an opponent's return is forced to be short, the point should be yours! A defensive clear incorrectly used in this situation would give the opponent time to move back and hit overhead, and the advantage would be lost.

The only difference in the production of these two types of clears is that the attacking clear has a flatter arc; therefore stroke it with less upward angle. It also requires less power, since without the height there is less distance to travel. Care must be taken when standing near the net that the flat clear is not sent out over the back boundary line. It necessitates controlled power and yet it has to be fast enough to get behind the opponent.

16

THE DROPSHOT (Figure 11)

The dropshot is a slow shot that drops just over the net in the opponent's forecourt. To produce it, use exactly the same grip, footwork, body position, and backswing described for the overhead clear. Indeed, your intention should be to suggest that a clear is forthcoming. The difference lies in wrist speed. There is still full wrist movement, but the shuttle is stroked with great control rather than "patted." The shuttle must be contacted farther ahead of the body than is the clear and with an

Figure 11—Dropshot

extended arm in order to direct it downwards. The downward movement of the arm coupled with the completion of the wrist action brings the shuttle down. In addition, the face of the racket is tilted downward at the angle you wish the shuttle to take.

A dropshot is invaluable because it enables you to use the front corners of the court. No other type of shot goes to the two front corners near the net. The smash and drive are placed midcourt or deeper, as shown in Figure 9. The clear is always placed in the backcourt; therefore, in order to make full use of the court and to move your opponent, the two front corners cannot be neglected. The dropshot, whether overhead, underhand, or hit from the side and from any place on the court, fills this need.

A major part of singles strategy is the use of the overhead dropshot in combination with clears. For example, if clears are used repeatedly, a player tends to move his basic position towards the rear of the court in order to cover the deep shots. This makes the dropshot very effective. Singles becomes a game of up and back and up and back again until a weak return is forced and a smash finishes the rally. A midcourt shot, one which is halfway between the net and back boundary line, obviously is not as useful in singles as in doubles, since these shots do not move the opponent out of center. Consequently, keep the shuttle as far from the center of the court as possible with clears and drops.

The most outstanding characteristic of a good dropshot is its deception. If the dropshot is deceptive enough it can be an outright winner even though it might have been planned as a lead-up shot. If it is obvious to your opponent that a dropshot is forthcoming, the play will not be difficult for him even though the drop has been accurately placed in a front corner. If your opponent is halfway to the net or at the net before your shot reaches the net, then you haven't fooled him!

The least attractive characteristic of the dropshot is its slow flight. Anything moving slowly unfortunately gives your opponent what you don't want him to have—time. The drop must be extremely accurate, then, to be effective. If your opponent anticipates the drop and has time to reach it, you have probably lost the exchange. It will take only a second for your adversary to get the shuttle back over on your side of the net. The dropshot then, contributes to the essence of the game—the selection of particular shots based on measuring time in relation to your own and your opponent's position on the court.

THE SMASH (Figure 12)

The smash is a powerful overhead shot used to "put away" any shuttle above the height of the net.

In the interest of deception, the smash should be masked as a clear or a drop. Use the same grip, footwork, body position, backswing, and contact point as with the clear and the drop, and your opponent will not anticipate your return. The smash differs from the clear and the dropshot in that it can be hit only from an overhead position; a clear and a dropshot can be either an overhead or underhanded shot. Be sure you move yourself to a position behind the shuttle as quickly as possible. Take care to have a proper body position, since balance must be perfect to achieve maximum power from your shoulders, arms, and wrist. The left shoulder must be turned to the net and the right shoulder back and ready to strike with force. The arm and wrist are cocked behind the body ready to unleash all available power. The racket head may be moving at a terrific rate as it goes out to meet the shuttle. The handle must be gripped quite firmly at the instant of contact, and the shuttle contacted at the highest possible point. The follow-through is down and in line with the flight of the shuttle. The overhead smash should be hit with as much power as that needed for the high, deep clear. To get such power, the wrist action must be full and the timing perfect. When you are first learning to smash, however, try to get your timing and downward angle correct before attempting to get excessive speed. Timing is thrown off if too much arm and body effort are involved in the stroke.

The racket face must be angled downward at contact point to make the shuttle travel sharply downward. It is important to remember that the farther away you are from the net the less angle to the floor you can get. Important, too, is that the farther you are from the net when you smash, the less speed your smash will have when it reaches your opponent's midcourt.

Figure 12—Smash

There are two reasons for using a smash. First, because it has more downward angle and speed than any other stroke, it is the main point-winning shot. If the pattern of play has developed as planned, your final stroke of the rally will be an overhead smash. Second, if the smash is returned, the return will be, because of the angle of your smash, an upward (defensive) stroke. Obviously, in both situations the smash is an invaluable weapon. There is, however, a reason for avoiding indiscriminate use of the smash; namely, the effort needed to smash leaves the body off balance, and therefore it takes longer to recover your position than with other types of shots. Moreover, repeated smashing is tiring and reveals weak thinking. So your judgment as to when to smash rather than to clear or to drop is important. Many factors related to you and to your opponent will enter into this decision.

It is interesting to note the characteristics which are alike in making the various shots. See Figures 10 and 11. The position of the feet and body is the same for all overhead shots. The stroke pattern—backswing, forward swing, and follow-through—should also be almost identical for the overhead strokes in order to employ the deception necessary to make the shots effective. What, then, determines whether an overhead shot is to be a clear, a dropshot, or a smash? The answer lies in the speed of the wrist, the degree of wrist action used, and the angle of the face of the racket at the moment of contact with the shuttle. On all badminton shots, cock the wrist back ready for the action that comes within the larger action of the shoulder and arm swing. Wrist power alone is not sufficient to propel the shuttle from one end of the court to the other; it necessitates arm and shoulder power in addition to exact timing of the wrist snap.

THE DRIVES (Figures 13 and 14)

The drive is a flat sidearm stroke played as a forehand or backhand.

The forehand drive is played on the right side of the body and is similar to the baseball sidearm throw. Take a forehand grip, turn your body until the left side is to the net, place the left foot diagonally forward, and turn the shoulders to allow the arm to take the backswing. The backswing is taken by placing the head of the racket between your shoulder blades. To do this, bend your elbow and cock your wrist backward in preparation for a big, full, powerful swing. Watch the shuttle closely with the idea of contacting it diagonally ahead of your left foot. As your arm and racket swing forward, your body weight should transfer from the right foot to the left foot, your wrist uncock, and your arm

20

straighten out at the point of contact. Contact the shuttle with a flat racket well away from you so that your swing is not restricted. The racket swings on through in the direction of the flight of the shuttle. The speed of your swing compels the racket to complete its follow-through by the left shoulder. The racket has practically made a 360° circle. The action of the swing, particularly in the contact area, is explosive.

The backhand drive employs the same basic principles as the forehand drive with two or three exceptions. The grip is changed to the backhand grip, making sure that the thumb is flat on the handle in order to give the extra support and snap that are needed. With this backhand grip there is less wrist action on the left side of the body and the wrist can be taken back only half as much as on the forehand side. The range of elbow movement is increased by this grip, however. This action of the elbow is important in this and all other strokes. On the backswing the elbow is bent, the right hand is by the left shoulder, and the elbow is pointing at the oncoming shuttle. The weight shifts, the shoulders turn, the arm starts swinging forward with the elbow leading, and then the head of the racket whips through for the contact and follow-through.

Long, deep, fast drives and slower paced midcourt drives can be played from either side of the body. Drives can be played like other shots, from one sideline diagonally across the court to the other sideline (cross-court) or they can be played parallel to the sideline (down-the-line). The flight pattern of the drive is parallel to the floor and just skims the net. See Figure 7. It is played anywhere from midcourt to backcourt and is driven to the opponent's midcourt or backcourt depending on his location in the court at the moment.

The higher you can contact the shuttle on the drive, the less you will have to hit up. For example, if you hit the shuttle from below knee level, it will have to go up to get over the net and will continue to rise as it carries on to midcourt. If it rises to net level and then turns toward the floor because the speed is lost, you have mistakenly hit a dropshot. Any shot higher than net level can be smashed and therein lies the danger of the hard hit drive played from a low contact point. One less powerful (midcourt) may be of value if the opponent is not pulled out of position. Its arc will reach its peak at the net and descend from there on to midcourt. It therefore cannot be smashed.

The fast drive is used when an opponent is out of position and you wish to get the shuttle behind him to the backcourt. Perhaps you hit a well-placed dropshot to his forehand. The deep backhand corner is now briefly open. If your opponent returns your dropshot to your forehand,

21

Can you send 5 consecutive overhead high clears to the area behind the short service line?

To the rear half of the opponent's court?

To behind the doubles service line?

Evaluation Questions

Figure 13—Forehand Drive

your problem is simple. If he plays it down-the-line to your backhand, it is not so simple. You must get the shuttle there quickly before he gains the center of the court or he will block the shot off for a winner while you are still recovering from the execution of the stroke. It takes more time to recover body balance and center position from hard hit power shots than from dropshots, midcourt drives, or net shots.

If the two kinds of drives are used correctly and intelligently, they can be valuable attacking weapons. Used badly, they can cause disaster.

THE BACKHAND CLEAR (Figure 15)

The backhand clear is a high, deep shot played from the left side of the court. Use the backhand grip with the ball of the thumb flat against the back bevel as described for the backhand drive. The feet and body positions are also identical with the drive. At the completion of the backswing, the elbow should be pointing at the oncoming shuttle.

Figure 14—Backhand Drive

The most important aspect of the swing is the timing of the wrist as it swings the head of the racket forward to meet the shuttle (at just the right instant).

For many players, the backhand clear from deep court is the most difficult of all the shots. Excellent timing and power are essential to clear the shuttle high enough and deep enough to make it a safe shot.

With all strokes, the learning process is the slow, gradual one of getting increased accuracy, further depth, and additional speed. As you continue to play and practice, the shuttle will travel increasingly more often in the direction in which you aim it. It will have more and more power in clears and smashes and less and less speed in dropshots. To further help you stroke your shots effectively and with care, correctly executed basic positions and footwork must precede the actual stroke production. The entire process, then, is one of smooth coordination.

Figure 15—Backhand Clear

3

Better Players
Master These Techniques

Additional strokes are fun to experiment with in combination with the essential skills described in Chapter 2. Descriptions of the half-smash, the round-the-head shot, the driven serve, the net shots (hairpin net shot, push shot, smash), and the underhand shots (clear, dropshot, drive) will be found in this chapter. Many of these strokes are no more difficult to execute than the basic ones, but the learning of them should not precede the mastery of sound basic strokes. Players who spend a great deal of time practicing the supplementary shots before mastering the fundamentals become chagrined when such practice fails to bring victory in tournament play. Often this dilemma is the result of dwelling on a spectacular, fancy shot or shots requiring less physical effort, rather than on standard, traditional shots which should be used the greater part of the time.

Nevertheless, as you gain experience and perfect your basic strokes, you will want to add the following accessory strokes to your repertoire. The value of employing these strokes is that they constitute a threat, that is, they could be used any time. The fact that your opponent must be alert to this possibility further assures the effectiveness of the basic strokes.

THE HALF-PACED SMASH

The half-paced smash, popularly called "half-smash," is simply a smash with less speed. The elements of stroke production related to the smash, described in Chapter 2 and Figures 7 and 9, apply to the "half smash." It is important to keep the following points in mind. The half-smash is played by contacting the shuttle with an extended arm diagonally above the head in order to obtain a steep angle downwards. To cut or slice the half-smash diminishes its speed and makes the shuttle fall close

Can you hit legal short serves (or long serves) on 5 out of 10, 7 out of 10, and then 9 out of 10 tries?

Evaluation Questions

to the net at a sharper angle. If the shuttle gets behind the player, the racket will be facing upward at contact point, the flight of the shuttle will be upward, and the shot will be a defensive one, in all probability a clear. It is important, therefore, that the shuttle be contacted well ahead of the body. Caution: a smash hit with a bent arm results in loss of power and angle. The smash is then known as a "flat" smash, a highly undesirable shot.

The half-smash has as many values as the full, powerful smash, but is of a different nature. The half-smash can be played with less effort. Moreover, it can be played from deeper in the court since recovery of balance does not present a problem. Moving to cover the net return after the half-smash can be accomplished with ease. By contrast, a full smash from the backcourt leaves the front corners vulnerable. The use of the half-smash therefore is less risky. It is valuable, too, because of its sharply angled downward direction. By hitting downward, the attack is gained by forcing the opponent to stroke upward. Very few points are won outright from an underhand stroke. The ones that are can be attributed to outright deception or to outpositioning the opponent.

THE ROUND-THE-HEAD SHOT (Figure 16)

The round-the-head shot is another overhead shot and an unusual one because it is played on the left or backhand side of the body. It may be a clear, a half-smash, or a dropshot. The execution of the round-the-head stroke is closely related to that of overhead strokes. See Chapter 2 for instructions. One major difference, however, is that the contact point is above the left shoulder, necessitating a reach to the left and a bend of the knees and body. The shot is played with the body facing the net and the weight on the left foot when the racket contacts the shuttle. The right leg swings forward for the follow-through of the stroke. The description and execution of the round-the-head stroke appear more difficult than the stroke actually is.

Figure 16—Round-the-Head Shot

Many sound reasons can be found for taking the shuttlecock with a round-the-head stroke rather than with a backhand stroke. First, more power is possible overhead than on the backhand, which, in turn, means better depth and speed on the shuttle. In addition, it is imperative to protect the backhand corner since the opponent will be attacking that area at every opportunity. The round-the-head shot meets this need. For example, if a low clear or driven serve to the backhand side can be anticipated, it can be intercepted with a round-the-head shot.

Not all the results of this shot are favorable, however, as the feet and body will have to be moved to the left side of the court to guard the backhand area, and a large portion of the forehand side of the court

Can you smash 5 out of 10 of your opponent's high serves to mid-court?

Can you smash 8 out of 10 clears received at midcourt or deeper?

Evaluation Questions

will be left open. Advantages gained by this maneuver will have to be weighed against disadvantages. The strength of your backhand and your speed of foot will be determining factors in selecting the round-the-head instead of the backhand. The ideal player will be able to play the high backhand shot as well as the round-the-head shot.

THE DRIVEN SERVE

The driven or flick serve is a fast, deceptive serve with characteristics of both the drive and the low serve. It has a low, flat arc that is just high enough and just fast enough to pass the opponent. See Figure 7 in Chapter 2. Note the fundamentals of stroking the serve and the drive described in Chapter 2. Apply these principles in the execution of the driven or flick serve. The intention of the preliminary movement, that is, the backswing, is that of the low serve until just before contact when the wrist is flicked into action. The flick is used in an attempt to deceive the opponent by adding to the speed of the stroke. The higher the point of contact, the flatter the arc can be. According to the rules, however, contact point must be below waist level and the racket head must be below the level of the hand at the moment of contact. These rules should be adhered to when practicing the driven serve so that the possibility of committing a service fault during the game will be lessened.

A weak return is the desired outcome of a good driven serve. Sheer speed and force of shot will not be enough for success. The deceptive element must be present. Very few points are won outright on the driven serve, or on any serve, since it is played from an underhand (defensive) position. If the driven serve can jolt your opponent off balance and thus place you in an offensive position, the immediate objective has been reached.

The mistake made by an ambitious receiver upon returning a good driven serve is to try to do too much with it. If the shuttle has carried behind the receiver as the server has planned it, the receiver should be content to play a safe, high, deep clear in order to regain balance. This serve will not be so effective if your opponent's speed of reflexes is exceptionally good. Against a player of different capabilities or against a player whose court position is faulty, the driven serve may be the answer to a serving problem.

The driven serve, most frequently used in doubles, has a specific value to a side-by-side (defensive) team. The angle that can be attained by serving from a position near the sideline can make an aggressive return almost impossible.

In conclusion, the effectiveness of the driven serve is due to its angle, speed, and some degree of deception. It must be noted here that the deception must be in the wrist. Any preliminary movements of the body intended to fool the receiver are illegal on the serve. This faulty tactic, called a balk, is further described in the rules in Chapter 7.

NET PLAY

Net play is a general term encompassing those shots played from the area around the short service line to the net. See Figure 7. Net play, which includes the hairpin net shot, the push shot, and the smash, is very important because the front of the court has to be defended.

The forehand grip described in Chapter 2 is generally satisfactory for net play, but the backhand grip must be adjusted slightly. The side of the thumb is placed up the back bevel of the racket which may cause a slight turning of the hand toward the forehand grip. The wrist is used differently for net shots, that is, with little relationship to the shoulders and body. This grip adjustment allows such wrist action. On the other hand, this grip could not be used successfully to perform a clear from the backhand corner. On both forehand and backhand strokes, spread the fingers and hold the racket almost loosely. This should give more "touch." To get even more control, hold the racket slightly up from the end. This shortening of the grip gives less power (not needed at net) and less reach. You must decide, therefore, what you wish to gain (control) and what you wish to sacrifice (reach).

The feet, body, and upper arm are used for reaching rather than for stroke production; the actual strokes are done with the forearm, wrist, and hand. The racket meets the shuttle with a flat face. The wrist action may be smooth and controlled or it may be quick, depending on the type of net shot you are attempting. The explosive power so essential for clears and smashes is not needed in the forecourt.

The follow-through should be in the direction in which you wish the shuttle to travel. Guide it and go with it. At times, the follow-through must be abbreviated to avoid hitting the net.

Your court position for net play in singles and doubles should be such that your extended arm and racket can just touch the net. Refer to Figure 17. This distance from the net will permit unrestricted movement of your arm. In doubles it will also enable you to cover more mid-court shots.

In net play take fast, small steps which allow you to turn and move quickly in any direction. The left foot should be forward on forehand shots and the right foot on the backhand ones. In exceptional cases, the right foot may be forward when that extra bit of reach is needed to get to the shuttle on the forehand side.

The most difficult shots to play at net are those which are falling perpendicular to the floor rather than diagonally. Diagonally dropping shuttles arrive farther back in the court; perpendicular falling shuttles, at their best, touch or almost touch the net as they fall toward the floor. These are extremely difficult to play, and since they cannot be directed forward, only upward, they are called hairpin net shots. Your opponent, sensing this, is alert to smash as soon as the shuttle comes up and over the net.

Figure 17—Net Shot

Hairpin Net Shot— The hairpin net shot gets its name from the flight pattern of the shuttle. See Figure 7. Played from one side of the net to the other, it should fall perpendicular to the floor and close to the net on the opponent's side. This

Evaluation Questions

Can you and your opponent keep the shuttle in play between the net and short service line for 6, 12, and then 18 hits in succession?

shot travels the least distance of any badminton shot; consequently, very little stroke is needed. The shuttle played at net level may be tapped or blocked back. Played well below net level, it will have to be stroked with great care up and over the net. Some championship players stroke the shuttle with a slicing action which gives the shuttle less speed and a spinning motion that is difficult to return. The perfect hairpin shot results in the shuttle's crawling up and over the net and trickling down the other side.

The Push Shot—The push shot is just what the name implies—a push, not a stroke. It is played at or above net level with the head of the racket up and the face of the racket flat. Its direction is angled downward. Refer to Figure 7 in Chapter 2.

The use of the push shot, almost nonexistent in singles, becomes highly effective in doubles. When a doubles team takes an up-and-back formation, the shot should be pushed down with a medium amount of speed to the opponent's midcourt. This will place the shuttle just behind the net player and force the backcourt player to reach and stroke the shuttle up. Confusion often results as to which player should return this shot. Obviously the push shot cannot be played from below net level.

The Smash—The other highly important net shot that has to be played above net level is the smash. The shot is accomplished by a downward snap of the wrist. It is the best return of a high, short shot; it is the kill! Care must be taken not to get excessively enthusiastic at the prospect of a set-up and bang the shuttle or your racket into the net. Instead, keep your eye on the shuttle and control your swing until the

Which strokes can you make from A, B, C, D, E?

Evaluation Questions
CHOICE OF STROKE

point is completed. The direction of the smash at this close range is not important. If it is directed straight to the floor with great speed, the smash will be unreturnable. See Figure 7.

Those net shots just described are used more frequently in doubles than in singles, but a good singles player's game is not complete without highly controlled net shots. A good net shot can be played by anyone— strength and height are not factors. Touch, deception, and quickness are the best qualities to have.

UNDERHAND STROKES

Underhand strokes are, like the serve, those in which the contact point and the head of the racket are below the level of the hand. Those described previously in Chapters 2 and 3 are the serve, the hairpin net shot, and the drive. See Figure 7. The outstanding characteristic of the aforementioned shots and those to be described here, the underhand clear and the underhand dropshot, is that the contact point below net level necessitates an upward stroke.

Underhand Clear—Many of the same stroke production fundamentals of the high, deep, singles serve—the grip, the footwork, the wrist and arm power, and the follow-through—can be applied to the underhand clear. When stroking this clear, the racket swings down from the ready position, under the shuttle for contact, and up, following through in the intended direction of the shuttle. Except for the fact that it originates near the net, the flight pattern the shuttle makes mimics the high, deep serve. Note Figure 7.

32

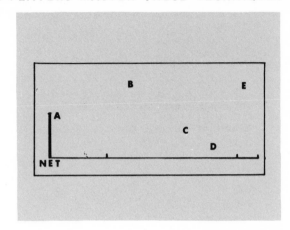

Diagram C:

CHOICE OF STROKE

Just as with the overhead defensive clear, the underhand clear is used to gain time to recover the center position and to force the opponent to the backcourt. Its values are many in both singles and doubles. For example, if a dropshot is not particularly good and does not fall close to the net, a large choice of shots is available. But near perfect dropshots necessitate a return with an underhand clear and the stroke becomes indispensable. The only alternative as a return of the perfect dropshot is the hairpin net shot.

Underhand Dropshot—The underhand dropshot described here is one played from an area between the short service line and the baseline to the opponent's side of the net and as near to the net as possible. It has specific use both in singles and doubles. Closely related, and yet different in its usage, is the dropshot played closer to the net, the previously described hairpin net shot. See Figure 8.

The fundamentals of stroking and the characteristics of the underhand dropshot are almost identical with those of the low serve described in Chapter 2. A slow, controlled shot, it has its limitations for this very reason. If it is played from the baseline at a slow pace, your opponent has time to pounce on it at the net. Unless it is disguised by "holding the shuttle" ineffective returns result. Although rarely played successfully from the baseline, its values are exceptional in doubles and mixed doubles when played from midcourt. In doubles, when employed to run the net player from side to side or to draw a player up when both partners are back, panic results. In singles, it can be a superb return of a smash. Directed crosscourt away from the smasher, it forces him to recover quickly and to run the long distance.

What strokes can be played from receiving points, A, B, C, D, E?

Which of these points require defensive returns?

Evaluation Questions
OFFENSIVE AND
DEFENSIVE STROKES

HOLDING THE SHUTTLE

The objective of all underhand shots, other than the serve, is to distract the opponent with deceptive moves. A phrase used often by badminton players, "holding the shuttle," refers to pretending to hit the shuttle before you actually do. For example, if when you pretend to play a dropshot, your opponent moves toward the net and you then flick the shuttle to the backcourt, you have "held the shot." This type of deception is generally employed with underhand shots. Deception on overhead shots results from preparing to stroke each shot identically as described in Chapter 2. You may hold the shot by a feint of the racket, head, or body. The "T" formation quarterback affords a good example of faking with the head, arms, and body. The open field runner often displays great deception to avoid the tackler. In badminton the same principle can be applied, although primarily with the racket. It takes time, however, to be deceptive. If you are running at full speed to return the shuttle, there is not time to produce feints! When you find the pace is slower and you have the time, reach forward to play the shuttle; then let it drop and contact it at a lower point. During the time the shuttle is dropping, your opponent may be committing himself forward or back. Be alert to this and either drop or flick the shuttle accordingly. If your opponent is moving too soon and getting caught repeatedly, he will be forced to hold his position until you actually contact the shuttle. Continue to watch the shuttle closely. You will tend to take your eye off the shuttle in order to see if and in which direction your opponent is moving. If your errors tell you that you are mis-hitting and indulging in needless fancy racket work, go back to the basics. If you can master this deception, however, it is a

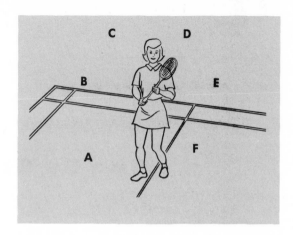

Diagram D:

OFFENSIVE AND
DEFENSIVE STROKES

tremendous weapon against a player who is very fleet of foot and likes to play a fast game. Slow the game down with defensive shots and then put your deception to work. Hopefully he will tire as a result; then you can apply your pace and power attack.

Using the strokes described in Chapters 2 and 3 in an appropriate sequence, you must outthink your opponent. Preconceived strategy and play are fine until you meet your equal or your supposed superior, in which case your thinking must be spontaneous. Your shots must have speed and control, and the decision as to the pattern or order they take must be made in the fury of the game. In singles, perhaps it will be two clears and then the drop, or clear and drop, and drop again; in doubles, a push shot, a smash, and another smash. In either game catch your opponent going the wrong way by not playing to the obvious open space; because he has moved to that obvious space, play behind him. Sometimes you may be caught in your own trap, but if your percentage of "catching" is greater than your percentage of being "caught," then you are ahead of the game. If your strokes are well executed and the rallies are long and the play interesting and close, then consider your game successful. That's the fun of the game. Mastery of the strokes will make it possible for you to delight in meeting a contemporary and pitting your forces against his. Play with enthusiasm and enjoyment. The winning and the rewards, whatever they may be, will be forthcoming. Reaching this stage of enjoyment comes as a result of concentrated practice. No amount of reading and thought off the court can substitute for hours of practice on the court. Both methods of learning, however, must be employed; therefore, the essentials of practicing will be discussed in the next chapter.

4

Progress
Can Be Speeded Up

The first step in learning badminton, understanding the why and how of stroke development, must be followed by actual stroke practice. No amount of intellectual grasp of the game can substitute for repetitive practice of the stroke pattern or for coordination of the racket and shuttle to assure correct timing. Mental and physical processes should work together to speed up progress.

Various drills and suggestions for the individual will be given in this chapter; group organization will be left to your instructor. For successfully executed drills, locate another student with approximately the same degree of skill; neither player benefits sufficiently if the range of skill varies too greatly. — — — — — — indicates path of the player.

OVERHEAD CLEAR DRILL (Figure 18)

Both players take their center positions where the drill for the clear starts with a singles serve and thereafter continues with clears only. The clears should first be played parallel to the sideline, then crosscourt, then alternating straight and crosscourt, giving each player a chance to clear from both deep corners. The shuttle should be directed repeatedly to the same corner before changing the direction to the other corner. The player stroking from the backhand should be using an overhead or round-the-head clear. The object is to repeatedly clear the shuttle high and deep from one corner to an opposite corner between the doubles and singles back boundary line. Returning to center position after each hit develops good footwork and stamina.

HINT: Get behind and in line with the shuttle for increased depth.

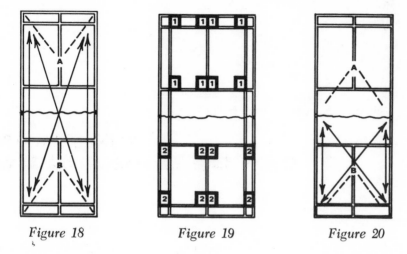

Figure 18   Figure 19   Figure 20

Figure 18—Overhead Clear Drill; Figure 19—Serve Drill; Figure 20—
Overhead Dropshot and Underhand Clear Drill.

SERVE DRILL (Figure 19)

Perfecting the serve, one of the easiest strokes to practice, can be done with or without a partner. To permit the server to take his service position for 20 strokes before retrieving shuttles, about 20 shuttles should be collected. This not only saves time but also adds to the consistency of the stroke. The serve, whether for singles or doubles, should be directed to a particular corner on the court. Even if a partner is present, the serve should not be returned; instead, it should be allowed to fall to the court, enabling the server to see exactly how close to the target the shuttle came.

HINT: Drop the shuttle well away from you in order to get the freedom of movement which will result in better accuracy.

OVERHEAD DROPSHOT AND
UNDERHAND CLEAR DRILL (Figure 20)

Both players begin in the center position from which the drill starts with a singles serve by A to a back corner. The receiver B returns it with an overhead dropshot to a front corner. An underhand clear to the same back corner follows and the drill continues drop, clear, drop, clear until one

37

Can you maintain each practice drill for four consecutive strokes?

player fails to return the shuttle. The shuttle should be directed repeatedly to the same corner until there is some degree of control before switching the direction of the shuttle to another front or back corner. Again, both players should return to the center position if the drill is to simulate game conditions.

HINT: Pretend to stroke an overhead clear and a hairpin net shot in order to acquire the deception needed for these two shots.

SMASH AND UNDERHAND CLEAR DRILL (Figure 21)

This drill, very much like the preceding drop and clear drill, begins with a singles serve by A to either back corner. A smash by B parallel to the sideline and to the opposite midcourt is returned with a high underhand clear. The drill then becomes smash, clear, smash, clear until either player misses; the drill then begins again from center with the serve.

HINT: Gradually increase the speed of your smash in order to eliminate faulty shots.

DRIVE DRILL (Figure 22)

There are four drives to be practiced: the straight (parallel to the sideline) forehand and backhand, and the crosscourt forehand and backhand. This drill begins with both players in the center of the court. One player hits a driven serve to the predetermined forehand or backhand of the opponent. Thereafter, repeated drives ensue: forehand to forehand; backhand to backhand; forehand to backhand; and backhand to forehand. Each of the four strokes should be practiced repeatedly before the side and direction are changed. Return to center after each hit.

Evaluation Questions

Can you send 3, 5, and then 7 consecutive overhead drop shots to the front half of the opponent's court?

To the area between the net and the short service line?

To within 3 feet of the net?

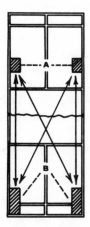

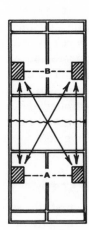

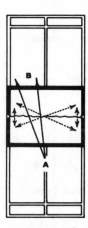

| Figure 21 | Figure 22 | Figure 23 |

Figure 21—Smash and Underhand Clear Drill; Figure 22—Drive Drill; Figure 23—Short Game.

HINT: Contact the drive high so that this drill does not become a smash, clear drill.

SHORT GAME (Figure 23)

This game, played and scored exactly according to singles rules, begins with a low serve by A and return of serve at the net by B: thereafter, only net shots, straight or crosscourt, can be played. Any shots, other than the serve, which fall behind the short service line are considered out of court. This drill, valuable to beginners learning rules and scoring, develops the skill and judgment in the forecourt necessary in doubles and mixed doubles.

HINT: Stand far enough away from the net to give yourself time and space to stroke properly.

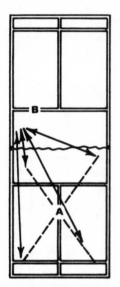

Figure 24—Unequal Partner Drill

UNEQUAL PARTNER DRILL (Figure 24)

Many times good players unable to find opponents of like skill can devise ways of utilizing beginners as practice partners. For instance, the advanced player A strokes the shuttle to one corner of the court to the beginner B who may then return the shuttle any place on the court. The advanced player develops control by playing the shuttle to the beginner's racket, thus enabling him to keep the rally going. The advanced player develops footwork, stamina, and stroke control chasing the comparatively uncontrolled returns of the novice. This drill can be amusing and fun to two players desiring to learn and willing to cooperate.

HINT: Enjoy the practice as if it were a game.

THREE STROKE DRILL

The first three strokes of a point, important because the offense or defense may easily be determined with initial strokes, should be practiced in that order and a decision made after each sequence as to the effectiveness of the serve, return of serve, and the third shot.

HINT: Try to be in an offensive position after the third stroke.

CONDITIONING

Whether a player is able to finish the match or practice period in good fashion, that is, still stroking the shuttle with power and control, is determined largely by his physical condition. The player in poor condition begins to make errors and to be slow afoot after a short period of time. Badminton should be a game of long, interesting rallies free from outright errors, and this demands strength and endurance.

40

Evaluation Questions

Using drives only, can you and your partner rally the shuttle 4, 6, and then 8 consecutive times?

There are various ways of improving one's endurance. Distance running, hockey, basketball—in fact, all the running games—are of value. Modern dance, gymnastics, and rope skipping add quickness and flexibility. Tennis and squash racquets, closely related to badminton, provide stroke needs similar to the badminton player's game. All these activities contribute to the conditioning process, but obviously the best conditioning for badminton is to play badminton. If the stroke practice drills are rehearsed properly with each player returning to center position between each stroke, endurance will be developed. Practice games against someone of exact equal ability will result in long endurance-demanding rallies.

Needless to say, smoking and alcohol negatively affect one's physical condition. Adequate sleep and food supply the energy needed to meet the demands of a strenuous game.

5

Patterns of Play

Certain tactics and strategy apply to all forms of badminton—singles, doubles, or mixed doubles. Tactics are "skillful devices for accomplishing an end," a "mode of procedure for gaining advantage or success." This chapter will discuss the tactics or strategy of badminton.

OFFENSE AND DEFENSE

An important aspect of badminton is the development of offensive and defensive play. Offensive strokes are point winners. They are shots which are directed downward—smashes, half-smashes, dropshops, half-paced drives, and low serves. Winning a point from an overhead position requires speed, sharp angles, and accurate direction. Defensive shots are those hit upward—clear, underhand dropshots, drives, and high serves. Winning a point from an underhand stroke has to be accomplished through deception or superior court positioning.

Offensive and defensive positions may change during the course of a rally. Defense can be changed to offense and vice versa, depending on how well a stroke is executed and selected for use at the proper time. For example, if the smash (offensive) is returned exceptionally well with an underhand hairpin net shot properly angled away from the smasher, and the net shot falls perpendicular and close to the net, the smasher is forced to hit up (defensive). If, however, the smash had been returned with an underhand clear or weak net shot, the offensive would have remained with the smasher. Offensive players take chances and strive for outright winners whereas defensive players are content to "play it safe" and wait for the opponent to err.

ANGLE OF RETURN (Figure 25)

The angle of return, as important in badminton as it is in tennis, is the angle the returned shuttle takes in relation to the court boundaries. It does not refer to upward or downward angle. Down-the-line and cross-court shots, with their varying degrees of angle, are commonly used in illustrating angle of return. To avoid being trapped by angle of return, position yourself on the court where the greater percentages of returns are likely to come. Occasionally you can neglect a portion of the court. This is the situation you strive for. For example, a high clear to your opponent's deep forehand (1) or backhand (3) corner can rarely be returned crosscourt high and deep to your diagonal corner because of the long distance. It could be returned with a flat, fast clear towards that corner, but you will be in the center (1 or 3) blocking it before it reaches the intended spot. A shot played to the center of the opponent's court (2) will make the center of the angle of return on the centerline (2). The best plan is to maintain your position in the center of the angle of possible return and then to be alert to the odd shot. Very few players can consistently play the odd shot successfully. It is generally a question of playing the basic fundamentals better than your opponent and understanding and applying strategic principles.

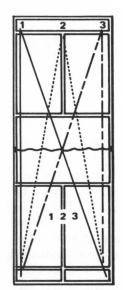

Figure 25—Angle of Return

CROSSCOURT SHOTS (Figure 26)

Crosscourting and angle of return are closely related. Crosscourt shots travel a long distance across the court, requiring considerable time for the shuttle to arrive at the intended spot. The "down-the-line" shot, a shorter distance, is the more logical shot and yet more obvious. For example, if you play the shuttle to your opponent's forehand side, anticipate the return on your backhand side. Of course, your opponent can crosscourt to your forehand side and must at times, but it will take longer for the shuttle to get there. You therefore will have more time to reach it. Your opponent will crosscourt and play the less desirable shot when he is on balance and can return to center quickly. He will also crosscourt when he discovers you have overanticipated. He too must be on balance when he discovers you have overanticipated. He too must be

43

Can you make your opponent move alternately forward and backward to receive your hits 5 times in succession?

7 times? 9 times?

Evaluation Questions

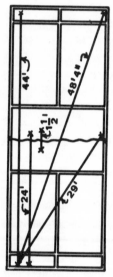

on balance when he crosscourts because he has put himself out of the center of his angle of return. A cross court shot of any kind played from forehand sideline to forehand sideline leaves the vulnerable backhand sideline exposed. If you decide to stay in the center of the angle and do not deliberately move to cover the down-the-line shots, then these shots become effective, even though obvious. Most of the time you should move about a foot to the side of the court to which you have directed the shuttle. If your shot has pushed your opponent to the back boundary line, you might move one step forward in hopes he will be unable to get sufficient depth from your good length.

Try to tray him by leading him into over-anticipating certain shots because you have played crosscourt or down-the-line shots in a specific pattern. Then, play the odd shot for a winner or to draw him away from a particular area. A player generally has a preconceived idea of how much he intends to use crosscourt shots and how to play each opponnent. As the game progresses, both players will be trying various plans in hopes of achieving a successful one.

Figure 26—Distance Difference

RECEIVING SERVE IN SINGLES (Figure 27)

Your ready position for the return of serve for singles and doubles is much the same as the ready position during a rally. Read the descrip-

44

Evaluation Questions

With one player using underhand and the other, overhead strokes, can you and your opponent rally the bird 6, 8, and then 10 consecutive times?

tion in Chapter 2 and note Figure 6. Variation in the body position is slight. Your feet in this case are placed comfortably apart with the left foot in advance of the right foot in a diagonal stance. This foot position allows an immediate push forward or backward. Serves are usually placed in the front or back corners (short or long) instead of to your side since the service court encompasses only half the width of the entire court. The ability to rush forward to smash the serve or to move back before the high serve gets behind you is imperative. Hence this diagonal stance allows you to reach the shuttle quickly on return of serve. As you take your position to receive the serve, place your feet in the diagonal stance and keep them stationary until the server contacts the shuttle.

In singles most serves are directed high and deep to the corners, and they force the receiver to back pedal quickly in order to get behind the shuttle for an effective return. See Figure 19. You should anticipate the usual direction of serves and adjust your waiting position accordingly by shifting your weight to one direction or the other in order to get a faster start. If, however, you overanticipate in either direction, the server is given the opportunity to surprise you completely with a change in direction or depth. Take care to keep your percentages on the return of serve in the proper balance.

Since the service court is shorter in doubles than in singles, stand closer to the net so that you can move forward to meet the shuttle at its highest point. See Figure 29. Just how close you can stand in doubles depends on your ability to move back for the surprise shot. If you are continually ineffectively returning the occasional high serve in doubles, then you will have to relinquish your forward post until your percentage of returns is satisfactory.

Whether you are playing singles or doubles, the general rule to follow is to change your position if you are encountering difficulties. Find the place on the court and the position which best suits you and best defies your opponent's plans.

SINGLES STRATEGY

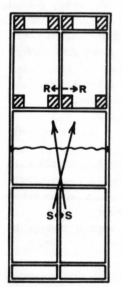

Figure 27—Receiving Serve in Singles

Singles can be described as a "running" game since it requires excellent physical condition to cover the 17 x 44 ft. area. Singles can be a difficult game for some players because it can expose weaknesses that might otherwise be covered up by a partner in doubles play.

The shots utilized most effectively in singles play are the high, deep serve, the overhead clear, the overhead dropshot, the half-smash, the underhand clear, and the hairpin net return. Occasionally a low serve, a driven serve, a drive, a push shot, or a full smash come into use, but these shots are reserved primarily for doubles encounters.

In singles, the point generally begins with the basic high serve. The low serve, occasionally used as a change of pace and to throw the receiver off balance, is a method of gaining the offensive since it may descend as soon as it reaches the top of the net and therefore cannot be smashed downward. See Figure 7 in Chapter 2. The more valuable high, deep serve moves the opponent to the back

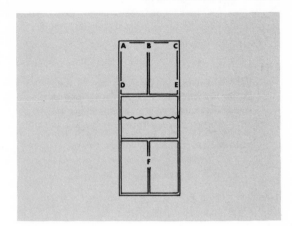

Diagram E:
ANGLE OF RETURN

boundary line to return it; a low serve, returned quickly, gives the server less time and permits the receiver to remain in the center position.

A clear to the opposite backline is the best and safest return of a long high serve. If the high serve falls short of even the doubles back boundary line, then a variety of returns can be played. A dropshot, a smash, a half-smash, or an attacking clear can be employed to gain the offensive; the choice depends on which one you can execute most successfully. This same theory holds true during the rally: shots of poor length can be dealt with more easily and with more variety than can serves or clears that fall perpendicularly on the back boundary line.

The general plan of attack in singles is to force the opponent to play a backhand from deep in the court. Most players, however, realize the vulnerability of this corner and conjure various defenses for it. The two most common defenses are using the round-the-head shot and moving the center position to the left. Consequently it is often better to open the attack to the forehand side, forcing the player away from the back-hand. A fast drive or attacking clear gets the shuttle to the corner quickly. Then you are sure to force your opponent to reply with a backhand rather than a round-the-head or an overhead stroke. The less time he has to play this backhand return the better.

Occasionally the weak area (backhand) is well defended and the strong forehand corner is neglected. In this case, a player's weakness may have become his strong point and his strength may have some flaws that can be attacked.

When the opportunity arises for your opponent to smash or play a dropshot, you must defend as well as possible. Midcourt shots have

47

Which team, A and B, or C and D, is in the offensive and which is in the defensive position?

What shots are used to attack the vulnerable areas of each team?

Evaluation Questions

DOUBLES TACTICS

little value in singles; therefore, the return must be close to the net or on the backline. Try to use your opponent's speed or angle to advantage and block or guide the shuttle just over the net with a hairpin net shot. Direct it the farthest distance from the stroker. For example, if he smashes or dropshots from the deep forehand corner, then your hairpin net shot should be to his front backhand corner. If your opponent anticipates the hairpin net shot and comes racing in toward the net, then flick a clear to his backhand corner. The next time this situation, the return of the offensive downward shot, occurs, go ahead and play the net shot. Alternate your pattern so that your opponent doesn't know what return to expect or just where to expect it.

Some singles players like the play to be as fast and quick as doubles, whereas others prefer to play a more deliberate power game. The shots characteristic of the quick player are the low serve, the driven serve, the flat clear, the drive, and the smash. The player who needs more time prefers to play the high serve, the high clear, the dropshot, and the half-smash. Many players are adept at both fashions of play and the use of a particular one depends on the opponent and the situation at hand.

DOUBLES STRATEGY

Doubles play, the most popular form of badminton, requires skill, wit, and cleverness. It is exciting, extremely fast, and demands excellent teamwork. It also requires less stamina than singles and is a game in which a weakness in a player's game can be disguised. The low serve, the driven serve, the drive, the half-smash, the smash, and the various net returns are all used effectively in doubles. Through various maneuvers

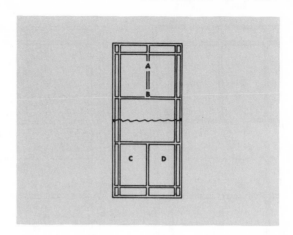

Diagram F:

DOUBLES TACTICS

by the two partners, a player may not have to use his less adequate stroke. Instead, both players combine their best assets. Partners unequal in ability can work out a combination that is unusually stable and effective. Four players, all of different skill levels, can combine and have great fun playing.

Three systems of doubles play are used most often. They are side-by-side, up-and-back, and a combination of these two. Men's and ladies' doubles teams use the side-by-side, up-and-back and combination systems; mixed doubles' teams prefer the up-and-back formation.

Side-by-Side or Defensive Formation (Figure 28)—A team in a sides formation (S & S) divides the court down the middle from net to back boundary line. Each player covers his half of the court, front and back. The basic serving and receiving positions for the sides team place each player in the middle of his half of the court. These positions, alterable as the situation changes, are defensive positions. The "down the middle" shots, those shots directed between the two players, are usually played by the player on the left side since it is his forehand side. A team with a left-handed player will discover some interesting advantages and disadvantages in its system of doubles play that will require some sorting out. It could be agreed that the stronger player is to play the middle shots regardless of which is his forehand side.

The advantage in using the "sides" system is that each player's area to defend is well defined and there is little confusion as to which player is to "cover" which shots. This defensive "sides" formation is the best system when you have been forced to hit the shuttle upward giving your opponents the opportunity to smash. With both players back from

49

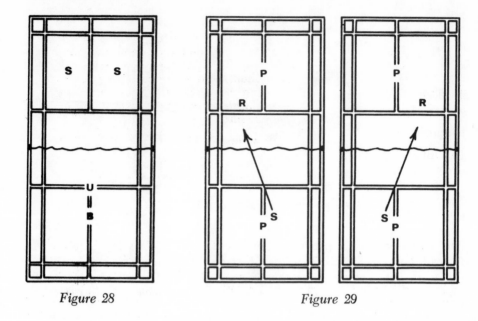

Figure 28   Figure 29

Figure 28—Side-by-Side and Up-and-Back Doubles Formations;
Figure 29—Up-and-Back Doubles Formations Serving to Right
and Left Courts.

the net, they have more time to defend against the smash and to cover
the areas (midcourt and backcourt) where a smash can be directed. The
disadvantage of the system is that the opposing team can play all the
shots to one side, up and back, and tire one player. If one player is weaker
than the other, the opponents will naturally launch their attack on him.

Up-and-Back or Offensive Formation (Figure 28)—In this system
the court is divided in such a way that when a team is on the attack, one
player plays the forecourt (U) and the other player (B) plays the backcourt. Note the serving (S) and receiving (R & R) positions for this
formation in Figure 29. The dividing line is about midcourt, depending
upon the agreement made by the two partners. (P)

The advantage of the up-and-back system is that there is always a
player at the net to "put away" any loose returns; this keeps the pressure
on the opponents. For example, as soon as one player can smash or drop-

Evaluation Questions

Can you and your opponent playing in "back" position rally the shuttle 4 times in succession, keeping it out of the reach of your partners as they play in "up" position?

6 times? 10 times?

shot from the backcourt, his partner moves forward to the net position to cut off any weak returns. Crosscourt shots can be more easily blocked with a player at the net. In addition, this formation makes it easier to protect weaknesses and to cover the part of the court to which a player's game is best suited.

The weakness of the up-and-back system lies in the midcourt area along the sidelines. The shot that is played just behind the net player and just in front of the backcourt player tends to cause confusion as to which player is to hit the shuttle. The resulting slight delay may prove disastrous.

Combination—The combination system is a means of rotating from up-and-back to side-by-side depending on whether a team is defending or attacking. The aggressive team will have to relinquish the up-and-back formation when either player is forced to hit the shuttle upward (defensive); therefore, when on defense, this team reverts to the side-by-side formation until it can regain the attack. The up-and-back formation is an inadequate defense against the smash because the player at net will not have time to defend, and his partner cannot protect the entire backcourt against a smash. The net player back pedals quickly to either side, preferably the closer, and his partner adjusts accordingly.

MIXED DOUBLES STRATEGY

Mixed doubles, played by men and women in the up-and-back formation, is a great attacking game and probably the one played most often at the club or in the back yard. It is superior to many games involving men and women because it is impossible for the man to concentrate his attack on the opposing woman with any degree of success. A more well-balanced game results in badminton than in tennis because the badminton net is at a 5 ft. height and the court is relatively small. For example, if the opposing man decides to smash the shuttle at the woman, she merely ducks below net level and lets the shuttle pass on for her partner to play. Because the court is not very wide, the man can cover it effectively.

See Figures 30 and 31 for serving and receiving positions in mixed doubles. The woman plays the shuttles in the front part of the court covering the short service line to the net. She should let clears, fast drives, and smashes pass her to be played by her partner who is responsible for most shots that arrive behind the short service line. The woman's objective in the mixed doubles combination is to control the attack by keeping the shuttle directed downward. This she does by using half-court and net shots. Such returns force the opponents to hit the shuttle up allowing her partner to smash. She will, of course, "put away" any "loose" (high and short) shots around the net. The man's objective is to play the returns from the back-court with fast, deceptive strokes which will force weak returns that can be severely dealt with (smashed) by his partner or by himself.

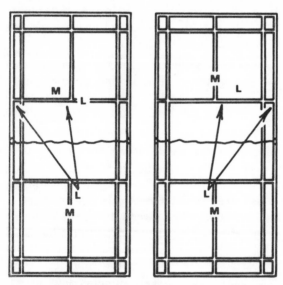

*Figure 30—Mixed Doubles Formation—
Lady Serving*

The low serve, always more offensively used in the up-and-back formation than the high serve, must be controlled with great care to keep the receiver from "rushing" the serve, that is, from pushing it quickly to midcourt or smashing it. If the serve is moderately good, the most effective return is the halfcourt shot to the backhand side between the two players. The return of serve should be just fast enough to hurry the opposing net player and yet not so fast that it carries beyond midcourt. The receiver playing this shot hopes the front player will debate as to whether it is feasible to take this shot, then decide against it and let her partner have it!

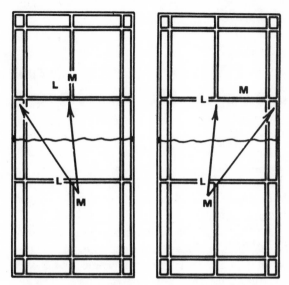

Figure 31—Mixed Doubles Formation—
Man Serving

By this time, the shot has dropped closer to the floor forcing a defensive return.

The court positioning of the two players, if incorrect, can be exploited. For example, if the net player stands too far from the net, hairpin net shots become very valuable. If she stands too close to the net, halfcourt shots become more valuable and the backcourt player has more court to cover. If the man attempts to play shots that should be played by the woman, his deep forehand and backhand corners become vulnerable. With cooperation and practice, a system can be developed that gets results and is enjoyable to both players.

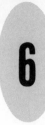

The Language
and Lore of Badminton

Modern sports often have peculiar, albeit fascinating, sounding terms. Pursuing the origins of the language of individual sports would doubtlessly provide many hours of interesting research.

For example, what explains the "side" of badminton's "side in," "side out," when there are never more than two players on one side of the net? A bit of investigation reveals that in its early years the game was played by sides consisting of at least three, usually four or five, players! Singles and doubles were nonexistent. Instead, a team consisted of several players who served in turn until they were individually eliminated. When all team members had finished serving, thus completing an inning, that group was said to be "side out." Currently the term "service over" is used in the official rules but players continue to say "side out."

Although singles and doubles are the accepted events in competition today, there are still countries, the majority Asian, where the many-sided game is still popular because of a surplus of badminton players, a lack of available courts, and a lust for long rallies which are, of course, prolonged because every inch of the court is covered by someone!

The derivations of the terms presented in the following glossary are equally fascinating, and pursuit of them by the curious student would promise interesting results. Some of them have been more fully described in earlier chapters of this book.

ABA—American Badminton Association. The national governing body in the United States was founded in 1936.

Alley—Extension of the court by 1½ ft. on both sides for doubles play. Referred to by the English as "tramline."

Back Alley—Area between back boundary and long service lines.

Badminton—The game we know today derived its name from the village of Badminton in Gloucestershire. It was here in the early 1860's at the Duke of Beaufort's estate that this new game, which was brought back from India by some Army officers, was first played in England.

Balk—Any deceptive movement which disconcerts an opponent before or during service. Often called a "feint."

Bird—The object with feathers which flies through the air over a badminton court in place of a ball. Parrot and eagle "birds" are popular in Thailand, bluebirds in Denmark. Officially known as shuttlecock. Commonly referred to as shuttle. (Figure 3).

Block—Placing the racket in front of the shuttle and letting it rebound into the opponent's side of the court. Not a stroke.

Carry—Momentarily holding the shuttle on the racket during the execution of a stroke. Also called a sling or a throw. This is an illegal procedure.

Center or Basic Position—Position in which a player stands in relation to the lines of the court, the net, the opponent, and the shuttle.

Clear—High, deep shot hit to the back boundary line. (Figures 10 and 15).

Combination Doubles Formation—Rotation of the side-by-side and the up-and-back formations. (Figure 28).

Court—Area of play. The size of the area bounded by the outer lines of play has not always had the same shape and dimensions. Although rules and regulations were drawn up as early as 1877 by Colonel H. O. Selby, Royal Engineers, and published in book form in Karachi, West Pakistan (then a part of India), the numerous different interpretations with reference to the size and shape of the court unfortunately delayed the development of the game. In the early part of the century in India the court was actually laid out on a ground about the size of a lawn tennis court, 78 ft. by 36 ft., and up to five persons played on each side (no wonder!). In England this confusion can be traced to the 1860's when the Duke of Beaufort introduced this glorified form of battledore and shuttlecock to his guests. The room in which the game was played had two large doors opening inwards on the side walls. In order to allow non-playing guests to enter and leave the room without disturbing the game in progress, it was decided to narrow the court considerably at the net, thus originating the 'hour-glass' shaped court. Variations of this peculiarly

55

shaped court were maintained for thirty years, and the first three All-England Championships actually took place under these trying conditions. Even in 1911 two English clubs, playing home and away team matches, found themselves playing first on a court 60 ft. by 30 ft., then on one 44 ft. by 20 ft.!

Crosscourt Shots—Shots hit diagonally from one side of the court to the other.

Deception—The art of deceiving or outwitting one's opponent. Accomplished in badminton with deceptive stroking by changing the direction and speed of the shuttle at the last minute.

Double Hit—Hitting the shuttle twice in succession on the same stroke. An illegal procedure.

Drive—A fast and low shot which makes a horizontal flight pattern over the net. (Figures 13 and 14).

Driven Serve—Quickly hit serve with a flat trajectory. (Figure 7).

Dropshot—Finesse stroke hit with very little speed which falls close to the net on the opponent's side. (Figure 11). In Malaysia the slowest type of drop is called the Coconut Drop because it falls perpendicularly. Described in this book as the hairpin net shot. (Figure 7).

Fault—Any violation of the rules. Most faults are broadly classified as either serving or receiving faults, or faults occurring "in play."

First Service—Normally used in doubles. Denotes that the player serving retains service.

Flat—The flight of the shuttle with a level horizontal trajectory. Also, the angle of the face of the racket which does not impart spin to the shuttle.

Flick—Speeding up the shuttle with a quick wrist action. Useful in stroking from below the level of the net, thereby surprising an opponent by quickly changing a soft shot into a faster passing shot.

Game—A game unit consists of 15 points in men's singles and in all doubles games; 11 points constitutes a game in ladies' singles. See "setting."

Game Bird—Game winning point.

Hairpin Net Shot—Stroke made from below and very close to the net with the shuttle just clearing the net and then dropping sharply downward. Takes its name, hairpin, from the shape of the shuttle's flight in a perfectly executed shot. (Figure 7).

Halfcourt Shot—Shot placed midcourt. Used more in doubles than in singles play, especially against the up-and-back formation. (Figure 9).

IBF—International Badminton Federation. The world governing body established in July, 1934, at which time badminton had become sufficiently world-wide in its appeal to warrant international organization. The IBF is governed by an annual meeting of the elected representatives of every national association in membership. One of its many functions is the management of the world famous international team competitions for the Thomas Cup and the Uber Cup.

Inning—Term of service. Time during which a player or side holds the service.

In Play—The shuttle is said to be "in play" from the time it is struck by the server's racket until it touches the ground or a fault or let occurs. See exception in Laws.

In Side—Side having the right to serve.

Kill—Fast downward shot which usually cannot be returned. A put-away.

Let—Legitimate cessation of play to allow an exchange or rally to be replayed.

Lob—A Clear. Term used principally by Malaysians.

Love—No score. English pronunciation of the French word "l'œuf" meaning goose-egg or zero. To start a singles match the umpire calls "Love-All, Play." To start a doubles match he says "Hand Out, Love-All, Play."

Love-All—No score. Also used after a game has been set. See "setting."

Match—Best two out of three games.

Match Point—Match winning point.

Net Shot—Shot hit from the forecourt with the shuttle just clearing the netcord. Hairpin net shots, push shots, and net smashes are the three most popular net shots. (Figure 7).

New York Badminton Club—Founded in 1878, the NYBC claims to be the oldest organized club in the world, although until the early part of this century it was more a club of social prominence than a center designed for badminton activity.

No Shot—Badminton etiquette requires a player to immediately call "no shot" when he has faulted by carrying, slinging, or throwing the shuttle.

"Out" Side—Side receiving serve: opposite of "in" side.

Point—Smallest unit in scoring.

Poona—Some historians believe the original name for badminton was "poona," the name coming from the city of Poona in India where a badminton-type game was played in the 1860's.

Push Shot—A gentle net shot played by merely pushing the shuttle without force. (Figure 7).

Ready Position—An alert body position enabling quick movement in any direction. (Figure 6).

Round-the-Head Shot—Stroke peculiar to badminton. An overhead stroke played on the left side of the body. The contact point is above the left shoulder. (Figure 16).

Rush the Serve—Quick spurt to the net in an attempt to put away a low serve simply by smashing the shuttle down into an opponent's court. Used mostly in doubles.

Second Service—Normally used in doubles. Indicates that one partner is "down," i.e., he already has had his turn at serving.

Serve or Service—Act of putting the shuttle into play. Opening stroke of each exchange or rally. (Figure 8).

Service Court—Area into which serve must be delivered, determined by the score. (Figure 19).

Setting—Method of extending games by increasing the number of points necessary to win tied games. Player reaching tied score first has option of setting. Further described in Chapter 7.

Set Up—Poor shot which makes a "kill" easy for the opponent.

Shuttlecock—(Figure 3). Official name for shuttle or "bird." The traditional shuttlecock, made with precious goose feathers and described in Chapter 9, is still used officially in all major competitions today. The first synthetic shuttle was made from plastic. More recently, nylon ones have been considerably improved and are popular in less important tournaments as well as in club matches. Shuttles have varied over the years. Early tournament players often had their choice between a "rocket" and a "slow wobbler." They continued playing with one shuttle until it lost several feathers as well as its original shape. Those used in the first few

All-England Championships were called barrel shuttles because of their shape. In early years unsuccessful efforts were made to produce fabric and papier-mâché shuttles. India tried making a substitute ball of Berlin wool wound on a double disc of cardboard 2½ in. in diameter with a central hole of 1 in., but it flew too fast.

Side-by-Side—A doubles formation. (Figure 28).

Side-In and Side-Out—See beginning of this chapter.

Smash—Hard hit overhead shot which forces the shuttle sharply downward. The game's chief attacking stroke. (Figure 12).

Stroke—Action of striking the shuttle with the racket.

Up-and-Back—Popular doubles and mixed doubles formation. (Figure 28).

Wood Shot—The shot which results when the base of the shuttle is hit by the frame of the racket rather than by the strings. Although they have not always been legal, the IBF ruled in 1963 that wood shots were acceptable.

Laws of the Game

The International Badminton Federation annually publishes a handbook containing the rules of badminton, officially termed "laws," as well as interpretations and revisions of these laws. Although an official handbook should be consulted for any tournament play, the following set of rules will suffice for scholastic and recreational play. The IBF has established laws pertinent to the court, equipment, players, toss, method of scoring, etc.

PLAYING SURFACE AND EQUIPMENT

1. The singles court measures 17 ft. wide and 44 ft. long; the doubles court measures 20 ft. wide and 44 ft. long. See Figures 1 and 2 in Chapter 1.
2. A net 5 ft. 1 in. in height bisects the court; the net posts are placed on the doubles sideline. The net dips in the center to a height of exactly 5 ft.
3. A detailed description of the official present-day shuttle will be found in the section on equipment. In order to insure the game's taking the same form whenever and wherever it is played, it is imperative to standardize a shuttle's speed. A profound difference in the type of game results if a fast shuttle instead of a slow shuttle is selected for use. The heavier the shuttle, the faster it flies. Each grain adds about four inches in length to its flight. The shuttle also flies faster under conditions of increased temperature and altitude. Weights of manufactured shuttles therefore vary from 73 to 85 grains in order to meet conditions at a particular time. Under normal conditions a 79 or 80 grain shuttle should be used. Each time the

game is played the shuttle should function at the same speed regardless of atmospheric conditions. The testing of a shuttle's speed takes place just before matches are to begin.

The test is made by having a player of average strength strike the shuttle with a full underhand stroke from a spot immediately above the back boundary line in a line parallel to the sidelines and at an upward angle. It is deemed correctly paced if it falls not less than 1 ft. or more than 2 ft. 6 in. short of the other back boundary line. See Figure 32.

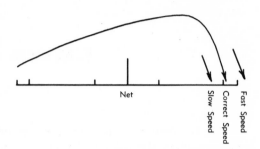

Figure 32—Shuttle Test

PLAYERS

4. Players are those persons taking part in the game: one player on a side in singles, two players on a side in doubles. The side which has the serve is called the "in" side and the opposing side, the "out" side.

TOSS

5. Before play begins, the opposing sides shall toss a coin or a racket. The winner of the toss shall have the option of serving first, not serving first, or choosing ends of the court. The side losing the toss shall then have a choice of the remaining alternatives. Decisions made at this time can be very important. One end of the court may be more desirable than the other because of lighting arrangements, floor conditions, and location of spectators. Outdoors, the wind and sun are major factors.

SCORING

6. Play is started by an underhand serve, and a side can score only when serving. (Figure 33.) Each time an exchange or rally is won while serving, one point is recorded. If the exchange is lost while serving, neither side is awarded a point. Instead, the right to serve is relinquished and the opposing side then has the chance to serve and score.

7. Doubles and men's singles games consist of 15 points; ladies' singles, 11 points. Peculiar to the scoring system is the term "setting." This is a method of extending the length of a game if the game is tied at a particular score. See the chart below.

Points in game	Score set at	Points required to win game
11	9 all	3 points
11	10 all	2 points
15	13 all	5 points
15	14 all	3 points

The side which reached the tied score first has the option of setting or not setting the score. If the side elects not to set the score, then the conventional number of points completes the game. A side which did not set the score at the first opportunity may have the opportunity, however, to set the score should the occasion arise again. In doubles, for example, if the score is tied at 13 all, and the team that reached 13 first declared no set, then play continues to 15. If, however, the score becomes tied at 14 all, which ever team reached 14 first is offered the opportunity to set the score.

8. A match shall consist of the best of three games. The players change ends at the beginning of the second game and at the beginning of the third game, if a third game is necessary to decide the match. In the third game, players shall change sides when either player first reaches 8 in a game of 15 points and 6 in a game of 11 points. The object of this change of ends is to try to give both players equal time on both ends of the court. If players forget to change ends, they shall change as soon as their mistake is discovered.

9. An inning indicates a term of service and there may be any number of innings since many rallies are played when no points are scored.

10. In doubles, each player on a team of two players is referred to as a server while serving his inning. First service is when the initial player is serving. Second service is when the other player serves. Service over occurs when both servers lose their serves. The side or team beginning a game has only one turn at serving in its first inning. Thereafter, both players on a side have a turn and both players take their turn in the innings.

PLAYING THE GAME

11. If a player attempting a serve misses the shuttle completely, he may restroke. An infinite number of attempts may be made provided the racket does not touch any part of the shuttle.

12. A serve is deemed completed as soon as the shuttle is struck by the server's racket.

13. After the serve is completed, players on both sides may take any positions they wish irrespective of boundaries.

14. A shot falling inside the boundaries or directly on a line is considered good.

15. In singles, players serve from and receive in the right service court when the server's score is zero or an even number. When the server's score is an odd number of points, players serve from and receive in the left service court.

16. In doubles, when their score is an even number, partners should be in the courts (right or left service court) in which they began the game. When the team's score is an odd number, then their court positions should be reversed.

17. The player or team that wins a game always serves first in the next game. At this point, in doubles, a team's serving order may be changed. For example, the losing team might decide that it could be more successful if a different player served first.

18. When any unusual occurrence interferes with the play, a "let" (replay of the point) can be invoked. This happens, for example, if a stray shuttle from a nearby court interferes, or if a linesman and umpire are unable to make a decision on a particular shot.

   The IBF has also established laws which cannot be violated without penalty. If any violation of the following laws occur, it is either point or side-out. In other words, if the receiving side errs, the serving side scores a point; if the serving side breaks a rule, no point is scored but it becomes side-out and the opponents then serve.

FAULTS DURING SERVING AND RECEIVING

19. A serve must be an underhand stroke and the shuttle must be contacted below the server's waist. To further insure that the serve is an underhand stroke, the entire head of the racket must be below the hand holding the racket. See Figure 33.

Figure 33—Legal Serve

20. A player's feet must be stationary and in their correct court upon delivery of the serve.

21. The server should not serve until the receiver is ready. If the receiver attempts to return the serve, however, he is judged ready. If a player is not ready, he should let the shuttle fall to the court and then tell the server or the umpire that he was not ready, in which case the serve shall be delivered again. This rule keeps the player who has a tendency to hurry his opponent from gaining an undue advantage.

22. No preliminary feints or movements to distract the receiver before he contacts the shuttle are allowed. A preliminary feint is any movement by the server that has the effect of breaking the continuity of the serve after the two players have taken their ready positions to begin the point. Such action is termed a balk, and a balk is a fault.

23. A serve that lands outside the boundaries of the service court is a fault.

24. A player may not serve out of turn or from the wrong court, and the receiver may not be in the wrong court. The consequences of an infraction of this rule depend upon when the mistake is discovered. If the player who commits one of these serving or receiving errors wins the rally, and the mistake is then discovered, a let is called. If the player at fault loses the rally, the mistake stands, that is, no let. If the mistake is not discovered before the next point commences, the already altered serving and receiving order is not changed until the end of the game regardless of which team won or lost the rally.

25. A serve may not be received twice in succession in an inning by the same player in doubles. If this occurs and a point is scored, the next serve is delivered to the other player.

26. The receiver's partner may not strike a serve meant for his partner.

27. If the shuttle falls outside the boundaries, passes through or under the net, fails to pass the net, touches the roof or side walls, or touches

a person or the dress of a person, the rally ceases and the player committing the fault is penalized. Some gymnasiums or halls may have low beams, ropes or other obstructions hanging over the court. In such cases the local association may establish a ground rule to the effect that a shuttle hitting the obstruction would not be considered a fault, but a let. If careful judgment by an experienced person is not made in this case, a player might intentionally hit the obstruction when it appeared that he was going to lose the point. If an obstruction can be hit deliberately, the fault rule is usually enforced. An unusual and uncommon situation develops when a shuttle passes the net outside of the net post and then flies into the court. This is the only case in which the shuttle can go below the net level and still be legal. It is most likely to occur outside on a windy day.

28. A player may not reach over the net to contact a shuttle. He may, however, contact the shuttle on his side of the net and follow through with his racket on the opponent's side, providing the net is not touched.

29. When the shuttle is "in play" a player may not touch the net or the net posts with his body, his racket, or his clothing. If he should hit the net following a stroke and after his shot has struck the floor, a fault does not result because the shuttle is not "in play" after it strikes the floor.

30. The shuttle may not be hit twice in succession before being returned to the opponent. This rule prevents setting the shuttle up to oneself or to one's partner.

31. The shuttle may not rest momentarily on the racket during the execution of the stroke. Commonly called "carry," "sling," or "throw," it is difficult to detect this fault, and it is often committed unintentionally by beginners because of poor timing. More advanced players seldom commit this fault outright, but occasionally when a deceptive technique is attempted the infraction may occur. When a "carry" is committed, the shuttle's speed and direction are changed. This naturally handicaps the receiver of such a shot, and a player should not be penalized by another's player's poor technique. The rule, then, is an essential one, and any player at fault should immediately call "No Shot."

32. A fault is called when a player is hit by the shuttle whether he is standing inside or outside the court boundaries. It is surprising to many players to realize that if they are able to hit their opponent

with the shuttle, the point is theirs! This, however, is more difficult to accomplish than it sounds.

33. It a shuttle is hit into the net or caught in the net on the striker's side, it is not "in play." If the shuttle goes over the net, a let results. The point is replayed since the player on whose side the shuttle was caught did not have a fair chance of returning the shuttle. If the player attempted to play the shuttle that was caught in the net and in doing so hit the net, then a "fault," rather than a let, would be called.

34. A player may not step on his opponent's side of the net even when, in returning a close net shot, he cannot stop his momentum until his feet are in his opponent's court.

35. A player may not bend down below the net and intentionally hold his racket above the net hoping that the shuttle will happen to rebound from his racket into the opponent's court. This occasionally happens when a player close to the net tries to defend against a smash. On the other hand, a racket held in front of a player's face for protection is a good maneuver and any resulting shot is acceptable.

36. A player may not "unsight" another player. This rule, applicable only in doubles, means that the server's partner cannot stand in front of the server in such a way that the receiver cannot see the shuttle about to be served. If this situation occurs, the receiver tells the server or the umpire, before the shuttle is served, that he cannot see the shuttle. An adjustment of the starting positions is then made by the serving side.

DISQUALIFICATION

37. Play must be continuous. A player violating this rule is not just faulted, he is disqualified. A player therefore may not leave the court, receive advice, or rest at any time from the start to the conclusion of the match. The umpire shall judge whether this rule has been broken and shall disqualify any offenders. Certain countries, where climatic conditions make it desirable, allow a five-minute rest period between the second and third games.

A thorough and accurate knowledge of the rules makes for a smooth, pleasurable game. Many misunderstandings can be avoided by the player who knows not only the rules but the reasons for them.

8

Unwritten Rules

Badminton, like all sports, has unwritten as well as written rules. The etiquette of badminton, which is basically consideration for other people, commences with your first introduction to the game.

First of all, attractive attire contributes to a wholesome atmosphere. Clean, white, comfortable clothing has always been the standard dress for racket sports and this unwritten rule should be adhered to regardless of a player's skill.

Certain standards should be followed when a club is organized in the neighborhood or at school. Members should be prompt in paying dues, attend meetings regularly, and assist in putting up and taking down the nets. Because of their expense, shuttles can present problems. Occasionally, club dues pay for their purchase and the person in charge of this detail must work out a system for their use which is fair to everyone. Usually, however, each player brings his own shuttles to club gatherings. In this case each player should contribute two or three new shuttles for the evening's play. If two players decide to practice at times other than regular club meetings, both players must make sure they arrive with plenty of good shuttles. In every club there are one or two players who always appear without shuttles or with ones of inferior quality. This type of person finds he is not invited to play in certain groups and often wonders why! If guests are invited to your court or club to play, the hosts should furnish all the shuttles.

During informal or competitive play, a player's personality may be disclosed, sometimes quite obviously, sometimes not. The quickness of the game brings out responses that are spontaneous, reflecting the character of the player. For example, a fault shot (carry, throw, sling) must be called before the opponent attempts a return. The player delaying the call "no shot" confuses the other players and the ensuing play. Another unacceptable way to make decisions—pretending not to know whether the shot was a fault—forces someone else to make a decision that is not his responsibility. The habit of continually suggesting that points be replayed when a player cannot make a particularly close decision is especially irritating. If, for example, every time a player places a shuttle on or near a line the opponent cannot make a decision as to whether it is in or out, even those shots that are well placed are nullified. Obviously this is discouraging to the accomplished player. Unsporting players who deceive themselves into thinking others are not aware of these finer points of etiquette establish unenvied reputations.

In informal play, the server usually takes the responsibility of calling the score after each rally. This eliminates many unpleasant discussions. Both players should keep the score to themselves even though they may not be responsible for calling it aloud. Keeping the score is valuable, of course, in planning the strategy for the next point.

In mixed doubles the man can demonstrate good manners in many ways. The lady usually serves first, crosses the net first when changing sides, and is consulted when any decisions are to be made. If conventional politeness is displayed between men and women both on and off the badminton court, no obvious display of manners is necessary.

Needless to say, emotional outbursts such as racket throwing and abusive language have no place in badminton and the customary absence of this type of behavior makes the game attractive to players and spectators alike. Even in the most highly competitive areas the sportsmanship is superior, perhaps even more so on this level. The champion must be a good example to others, particularly to youngsters, who emulate the winner in every way.

Some unwritten etiquette procedures apply specifically to the tournament player, but beginners and club players may find them useful also. When entering a tournament, the player should fill out his entry accurately, supplying all the information requested. This is a distinct advantage to the tournament committee responsible for making the draw, scheduling the matches, housing the players, and publicizing the tournament. The entry blank should be returned no later than the date requested. Players should not expect tournaments to accept late entries and should not protest when they are not accepted. Upon arriving at the scene of the tournament, the entrant should report immediately to the committee in charge in order to determine the time and court number for his match. The default time of fifteen minutes should not be extended by the player at any time.

A player should find out whom he is to play and should introduce himself to his opponent if they have not previously met. A friendly attitude should prevail between opponents from the start until the conclusion of their association.

Prior to the warm-up period, a shuttle suitable to both players should be tested and selected. During the warm-up time, the shuttle should be kept in play in order to give the opponent a fair chance to move around and hit the shuttle a sufficient number of times. Be sure your opponent is ready before you serve to him and be ready yourself when he is ready to serve. Retrieve shuttles that fall in your court and those on your opponent's side by the net if you are closer. Return the shuttle directly to the server, not just anywhere in his court. If a shuttle becomes damaged during play, it is courteous to ask your opponent if a change of shuttle can be made. An occasional compliment, "fine shot," on your opponent's winning stroke has always been acceptable! Maintain a spirit of fairness and generally it will be reciprocated. In addition, play your best; careless play is an insult to your opponent.

Following the completion of a match a player should always shake hands and, depending upon the outcome of the match, either congratulate his opponent on winning or thank him for playing the match. He should always thank the umpire too, and then report the score to the official table and inquire as to the time of his next match.

Learn to win and lose gracefully. It is unnecessary to expound on your victories; any good play will be noticed. A defeat should not be blamed on a minor or trivial matter, nor should excuses be found for poor play. Instead keep your thoughts to yourself, analyze the match, and determine to do better the next time.

The final obligation of a gracious tournament player is to write thank-you notes to the tournament or school officials and to the people who have shown special courtesies such as supplying housing and meals. This detail must be attended to promptly and is equally as important as sending in the original entry.

9

Facts for Enthusiasts

A racket, a shuttle, and a court with a net are all that are really needed to play badminton. Fortunately, this equipment is readily available and relatively inexpensive. Complete sets which include all the necessary equipment are available in most sporting goods stores, or each item can be purchased separately. Since a racket is the most important item of equipment, novices should ask an experienced person to help in its selection. Try several rackets, finally choosing the one which has the correct balance and a grip that feels comfortable. No rules or specifications govern the size of the racket. It may be any length or weight a player desires. Manufacturers have arrived, however, at a standard size which is 26 in. in over-all length; approximately 10 in. is in the head, 11 in. in the shaft, and 5 in. in the grip. The balance point is the mid-point or 13 in. from either end. Rackets weigh from 5 to 5½ ounces.

Until recently rackets were made entirely of wood, but now quality ones are usually constructed from hickory wood with a steel or fiberglass shaft. A good racket will cost about $18.00 but one entirely suitable for school and recreational play can be purchased for $6.00. The racket can be strung with lamb's gut or nylon strings. Tournament players like tightly strung rackets with qood quality gut. A tightly strung racket will "ping" while one strung too loosely will have a "plud" upon contact with the shuttle or when strummed with the fingers. Nylon strings are less expensive than gut and are perfectly adequate for club and school use. This type of string is resistant to moisture and maintains its playing qualities from one season to the next.

To prevent warping, rackets should be kept in a press when not in use and the screws on the press should exert equal pressure on the racket frame. A laminated racket frame is less apt to warp than a single piece of wood. The tighter a racket is strung the more likely it is to warp. To keep rackets and strings in top condition, they should not be stored in exceptionally damp or dry places.

The selection of a shuttle will depend upon the amount of money available and the objectives of the player. The feathered shuttle used most often in tournament play is the most fragile, the most expensive and requires the most care. It must weigh from 73 to 85 grains and have 14 to 16 feathers attached to a kidskin covered cork base. The feathers should be from 2½ to 2¾ in. in length from the tip of the feathers to the cork base. The feathers should flare at the top from 2⅛ to 2½ in. These specific requirements give the shuttle its unusual, although entirely predictable, flight patterns which are quite different from those of a ball. Synthetic shuttles are manufactured exactly to the foregoing specifications except that the feathers are of nylon and made in one piece. A good synthetic shuttle costs about as much as a feathered shuttle, 65 to 75 cents, but it lasts many times longer.

Proper care of shuttles, particularly the feather ones, is vital to preserving them and extending the length of time they can be used. Feathered shuttles come in tubes with instructions as to the humidity necessary to prevent drying and the resultant breaking of feathers. Any time a feather becomes ruffled, it should be smoothed out. Obviously, any action that would damage or break the feathers should be avoided. Although synthetic shuttles with nylon feathers are more durable, prudence should be shown in storing and handling them too.

Nets and net posts are essential for play. The least expensive net costs about $2.50. The official tournament net is priced at $11.50. The price of net posts ranges from $4.00 to $85.00. The top-priced posts are excellent for club or school use and are light weight aluminum posts with floor plates fixed permanently in the floor.

10

Playing the Game

Although badminton is still considered a minor sport in the United States, there is evidence that it is becoming increasingly popular. It is played in back yards, schools, and clubs, and there are a variety of competitions for all players.

The governing body of the sport in the United States is the American Badminton Association. The A.B.A. governs the six badminton regions of the United States, which in turn administer the activities of the state associations and their member clubs. Any member of an affiliated club automatically becomes a member of the A.B.A. Clubs usually meet at a school, a Y.M.C.A., or at a club especially built for badminton. Any person who wishes to play in a tournament sanctioned by the A.B.A. must belong to a member club. Most tournaments, with the exception of school events, are sanctioned. A list of clubs and their addresses is published in *Bird Chatter,* the official quarterly publication of the A.B.A.

Many tournaments (all indoor) are available to the interested amateur competitor. Each region has a tournament chairman who organizes and schedules the events in his region. Information regarding the chairman and the schedules can be found in *Bird Chatter.* At present there are club, state, regional, and national amateur championships. National championships are held for men and women in singles, doubles and mixed doubles, in the several age-based divisions.

The International Badminton Federation, founded in 1934, is the organization that governs the sport internationally. It consists of 46 affiliated national badminton associations, one of which is the A.B.A., which joined in 1938. Thirty-one years before the I.B.F. came into being, the first mixed team match took place between England and Ireland.

Since that time more than 35 countries around the world have participated in similar matches. Denmark, England, Indonesia, the United States, West Germany, and Malaysia are the most active international participants.

The All-England Championships is the oldest and most famous badminton tournament in the world, and it always attracts entries from many countries. It was first held in 1899, and it has grown so in strength and importance almost every year since that play now is always witnessed by thousands.

The Swiss Badminton Federation instituted the Helvetia Cup in 1961-62; it provides team matches among Austria, Belgium, France, Netherlands, West Germany, and Switzerland.

The Nordic Championships, started in 1962-63, are individual matches played annually by representatives from Denmark, Finland, Norway, and Sweden. In 1962 badminton was officially introduced into the Asian Games (contested every four years). In August of 1966 the game will be introduced into the British Empire and Commonwealth Games at Kingston, Jamaica.

The Thomas Cup is competed for triennually by men from countries that are affiliated with the I.B.F. Sir George Thomas, founder-president of the I.B.F., donated this renowned trophy for international competition among men's teams. The matches are composed of five singles matches and four doubles matches. To date, Malaya and Indonesia each have won the trophy three times.

The Ladies International Badminton Championship for the Uber Cup is also held triennually. The team trophy was donated by one of England's greatest players, Mrs. H. S. (Betty) Uber. The United States has held the Cup since its inauguration in 1957. The 1965-66 competition for the Cup was held throughout the world, with the challenge round in New Zealand.

Selected References

BOOKS

Davidson, Kenneth, and Lealand Gustavson. *Winning Badminton*. New York: The Ronald Press Co., 1953.

Davidson, Kenneth, and Lenore Smith. *Badminton*. Sterling Publishing Co., Inc., 419 Fourth Ave., New York 16, N.Y.

Davidson, Kenneth, and Lenore Smith. *How to Improve Your Badminton*. The Athletic Institute, 209 South State St., Chicago 4, Illinois, 1952.

Mott, Jane A. Chapter 3 "Badminton" in *Individual Sports for Women*, 4th ed. (Ainsworth, Dorthy et al), Philadelphia: W. B. Saunders Co., 1963.

MAGAZINES AND GUIDES

Badminton Gazette, official publication of Badminton Association of England, 4 Madeira Avenue, Bromley, Kent, England.

Bird Chatter, official publication of the American Badminton Association, Grace Devlin, Dolfield Rd., Owings Mills, Md.

International Badminton Federation Handbook, H.A.E. Scheele, 4 Madeira Avenue, Bromley, Kent, England.

Official Rules, American Badminton Association, D. Richardson, 20 Wamesit Road, Waban, Mass.

Tennis-Badminton Guide, Division for Girls and Women's Sports, American Association for Health, Physical Education and Recreation, 1201 Sixteenth Street, N.W., Washington, D.C.

FILMS (16 mm)

Beginning Badminton Series, Athletic Institute, Merchandise Mart, Room 805, Chicago 54, Illinois.

Fundamentals of Badminton, All American Productions, P.O. Box 801, Riverside, California.

Let's Play Badminton, General Sportscraft Co., Ltd., 33 New Bridge Road, Bergenfield, N.J.

Index

ABA, 54, 72, 74
All-England Championships, 73
alley, 54
angle of return, 7, 43
attacking clear, 16

backhand clear, 23-24
backhand drive, 10, 13, 20-21, 23
back pedaling, 9
Badminton, 1-4, 55, 72
balk, 55, 64
bird, 55
block, 55, 66
books, 74

carry, 55, 65, 67
center position, 7, 55
combination doubles, 51, 55
conditioning, 40-41
court, 2, 55, 60
crosscourt shots, 43-44, 56

deception, 18, 28, 34, 56
defense, 42
defensive clear, 16
defensive doubles, 49
disqualification, 66
double hit, 56, 65
doubles, 1-3, 62-63
doubles strategy, 48-51
drills, 36-40
drive drill, 38
driven serve, 28-29, 56
drives, 10, 13, 20-23, 56
dropshot, 10, 13, 17-18, 37, 56
dropshot and clear drill, 37

equipment, 70-71
etiquette, 67-69

fault, 56, 63-66
films, 75
first service, 56, 62-63
flat, 20, 56
flick, 28, 56
flight patterns, 10
footwork, 9-11
forehand drive, 10, 13, 20-22

game, 1-4, 56, 62-63, 72-73
game bird, 56

glossary, 54-59
grips, 5-6

hairpin net shot, 10, 13, 30-31, 56
halfcourt shot, 57
halfsmash, 10, 13, 25-26
Helvetia Cup, 73
holding the shuttle, 34

IBF, 57, 60, 72-74
inning, 57, 62
in play, 3, 57, 65-66
"in" side, 57, 61

kill, 57

legal serve, 11, 63-64
let, 57, 63-64
love, 57

magazines, 74
match, 1, 57, 62, 68-69
mixed doubles strategy, 51-53

net, 1, 60, 71
net play, 29-32
net shots, 10, 13, 57
Nordic Championships, 73
no shot, 58, 65, 68

offense, 42
offensive doubles, 50
"out" side, 58, 61
overhead clear, 10, 13-16, 36-38
overhead clear drill, 36-37

placement areas, 13
players, 61
playing surface, 60
point, 1-3, 58, 62
push shot, 13, 31, 58

racket, 3, 70
ready position, 7-8, 58
receiving faults, 64
receiving serve, 44-46
round-the-head shot, 26-27, 58
rules, 60-66

scoring, 1-3, 61-63
second serve, 58, 62

77

INDEX